Chasing
Jonah

A Mission 119 Guide to Jonah

Hutson Smelley

Chasing Jonah

Unless otherwise indicated, Bible quotations are taken from The King James Bible.

ISBN: 978-0-9861336-2-6

www.proclaimtheword.me

This volume of the Mission 119 Series is dedicated to Dr. G. Harry Leafe (1940-2015), whose teaching ministry inspired so many to pursue a deeper knowledge of the Word of God and always run to win.

Other Works by the Author

Better with Jesus: A Mission 119 Guide to Hebrews (2015)

Love, Romance and Intimacy: A Mission 119 Guide to the Song of Solomon (2016)

Living Hope: A Mission 119 Guide to First Peter (2019)

Deconstructing Calvinism - Third Edition (2019)

Looking Forward, Living Now: A Mission 119 Guide to Zechariah (2020)

Table of Contents

Preface to the
Mission 119 Series

The psalmist declares, "Thy word is a lamp unto my feet, and a light unto my path." (Psalm 119:105) The Bible is unlike all other books, not only in its grandeur and scope, but because its words are God's Words. The Bible presents to us God's special revelation of Himself, His biased view of history past and future, the reality of who we are, and a picture of all that we can be. Woven within its pages and spilling over is God's redemptive plan for humanity, with Jesus Christ as centerpiece. We do not study the Bible merely to accumulate head knowledge, but with the earnest expectation of knowing God more and drawing near to Him. Each page has something for us, sometimes encouraging us, sometimes reproving us, always revealing God, and every jot and tittle a precious morsel for our souls. Against the backdrop of a world encased in darkness, it is the light of truth that pierces through all the deceptions and puts reality in clear focus.

Every generation faces challenges, and the present generation is challenged about truth and whether any absolute truths are knowable. Like all the ones before it, this generation needs to hear God's Word taught boldly, with clarity, without apology, in grace and love. And this generation needs to be reminded by those who teach that the Bible was written for everyone. God has spoken with clarity so that all believers who come to the Bible yielded to what God has for them can know its truths as they grow and mature. The aim here is to strike the proper balance between too little detail to elucidate the message and superfluous detail that obscures, so that this volume is accessible and profitable to laypersons and teachers alike who seek to understand the author's original intended meaning and the continuing relevance of that message today. With this in mind, the Mission 119 Series is designed to provide guidance for the understanding and exposition of books of the Bible with depth and a commitment to a plain sense interpretation tethered first and foremost to the context and flow of argument of the book under consideration.

A common sentiment today is that people need only "relevant" teaching from the Bible, which suggests portions of the Bible are irrelevant, and too often means they want three steps to raising teens in place of the perfections of God, five steps to a better marriage in place of how a believer matures and walks in the Spirit, how to find blessing and wealth in place of God's demand for holy living, and so forth. May I say that every word God ever spoke was relevant and remains so today. Those who would step forward as teachers of the Word of God only do people a disservice by trying to conform God's Holy Word to the world's bankrupt self-help counterfeits when what is most needful today is the plain teaching of the whole Bible as it is. Believers engaged in the Word and yielding to the Holy Spirit will find the most practical of wisdom and grace enablement for all areas of their lives as they draw near to God in the transformative experience of knowing Him more and more. May I also suggest that while some people will flee teaching that has depth and conviction, far more people in churches today are thirsty for more depth in the teaching. They want to see that the Bible is not clichés and recycled sugar sticks but truly a light from God unto their paths. In this vein, it is my prayer that this volume of the Mission 119 Series will be a useful guide for teachers of the Bible and a special blessing for students of the Word who aspire to know God more.

Chapter 1

Introductory Matters

If there is a portion of Scripture most disregarded today, it may well be the so-called Minor Prophets. The Minor Prophets refers to the 12 books of the Bible from Hosea through Malachi, and they are termed "minor" because of their shorter length relative to the prophetic writings of Isaiah, Ezekiel and Jeremiah. Yet as with all of the Bible, we find great riches in these shorter writings. And by the same token, much is lost if we forsake these writings. Although written in the context of discussing the Old Testament in general, the eloquent words of David Baron in the preface to his *Rays of Messiah's Glory* are apropos here:

> What is needed with regard to this is, not argument or persuasion, but relish and appetite—the symptoms of vigorous spiritual health which, alas! As far as the majority of professing Christians are concerned, is sadly wanting. It is only a shallow and sentimental piety that will pick and choose from the Word of God and declare itself satisfied with certain portions of it only, to the neglect and

depreciation of the rest; and if Christians will thus insist on abstaining from partaking of the *variety* of food which God has graciously, in His infinite wisdom, provided for the sustenance of their spiritual life, of course they have only themselves to blame of their loss of spiritual vigour and the setting in of moral decrepitude, which in time makes not only service, but even the partaking of the "fat things" which are provided for them in the Word of God, at best a wearisome *duty* instead of a privilege and pleasure.[1]

To this, we may add, as Charles Feinberg aptly remarked: "Amazing it is how timely and applicable are the messages of these servants of God for our distraught age. He who would be well balanced in the truth of God must ponder these words of the prophets."[2]

The New Testament made frequent use of the Minor Prophets by quotation and allusion. (e.g., Jesus' references to Jonah in Matthew 12:40-41, 16:4; Paul's quotation from Habakkuk 2:4 in Romans 1:17) When Philip searched out Nathanael to announce he had found the Messiah, he said, "We have found him, of whom Moses in the law, and the prophets, did write, Jesus of Nazareth, the son of Joseph." (John 1:45) And indeed, when Jesus spoke of himself to the disciples on the Emmaus Road: "And beginning at Moses and all the prophets, he expounded unto them in the scriptures the things concerning himself." (Luke 24:27) These ancient writings to ancient peoples still point to Jesus

---

[1] Baron, David, *Rays of Messiah's Glory* (Eugene: Wipf and Stock Publishers, 2001), 7-8.

[2] Feinberg, Charles L., *The Minor Prophets*, Moody Publishers (1976), p. 132.

and continue to wield the sharp edge of truth today. In this modest work, I hope the reader will find these comments borne out by the little book of Jonah, and be encouraged to plumb the depths of all the writing Prophets.

A Maligned and Misunderstood Book

While the book of Jonah is likely the best known among the Minor Prophets, it has suffered critical attacks from those that dispute its historicity and widespread misunderstanding from those who accept its historicity. The critical attacks unrelentingly question not only the general historicity (e.g., whether Jonah went to Nineveh and whether the Ninevites repented) but also all of the miraculous or supernatural elements (e.g., the fish of chapters 1-2, the gourd plant of chapter 4). Indeed, "[d]isbelief has attacked this book probably more than any other in the Bible."[3] Feinberg rightly observed: "Ridicule has especially centered around the swallowing of Jonah by the fish and his preservation in it. The root of the difficulty is the denial of the miraculous. But if we exclude the miraculous from our Bibles, how much of it do we have left? And more important, what kind of God do we have left? It is nothing less than shortsighted unbelief to think that the difficulty is solved by the removal of this miracle from the book of Jonah."[4] Sadly, these criticisms have caused many to miss the richness of the book. The New American Commentary volume on Jonah said it well: "The character, Jonah, has intrigued believers for many centuries. Unfortunately, he has become caricatured by many who miss the positive results of an objective examination of his life. The Book of Jonah is a

---

3 Feinberg, Charles L., p. 133.
4 Feinberg, Charles L., p. 134.

case study of 'missed blessings' because so many readers focus upon its supposed difficulties rather than upon its rich teachings."[5]

The story that unfolds in the text is not too difficult—and I loosely refer to the "story" because Jonah reads in many ways like a story. As Chisholm explained, "The Book of Jonah differs from other Minor Prophets in that it is an account of the prophet's experiences, rather than a collection of prophetic speeches."[6] The IVP Dictionary similarly expressed the uniqueness of the book of Jonah:

> The book of Jonah is unusual among the prophets because it recounts a story about the prophet himself rather than mainly preserving the words that he preached. Typically, the OT Prophetic Books do the latter; they provide little or no biographical information about the prophet whose name they bear, but they do preserve the text of the message that he was inspired to preach. In the case of Jonah, only five Hebrew words that he preached to the people of Assyria are preserved, those that are translated as 'Forty days from now Nineveh will be overthrown' (Jon 3:4).[7]

This is not to say that detailed biographical content is unheard of. Most notably, the book of Daniel contains substantial content about his life. The difference is that

---

[5] Billy K. Smith and Franklin S. Page, *Amos, Obadiah, Jonah*, vol. 19B, The New American Commentary (Nashville: Broadman & Holman Publishers, 1995), 203.

[6] Chisholm, Robert B., Jr., *Interpreting the Minor Prophets*, Academic Books (1990), p. 119.

[7] Mark J. Boda and J. Gordon McConville (eds), *Dictionary of the Old Testament Prophets* (Downers Grove: InterVarsity Press 2012), 455.

Daniel contains a balance of biographical content and his prophetic words. In contrast, Jonah is dominated by biographical content.

Jonah's experiences are intriguing, and perhaps most of all due to the swallowing of Jonah by a great fish, the "story" of Jonah is well known. In fact, "Jonah is one of the Bible's best-known characters. Even strangers to most biblical content have heard about Jonah and the 'whale.'"[8] But should we understand the story as history, allegory or something else? And regardless of the genre we assign to Jonah, what is its core teaching? It has been observed that "[t]he Book of Jonah is perhaps the most misinterpreted book in the Bible."[9] Some take it as allegory or parable, leading to disparate and unverifiable (sometimes fanciful) interpretations, while many that affirm its historicity write into the text a New Testament missionary message belied by the fact that outside of Jonah, other Old Testament prophets seldom went beyond the borders of Israel. These views will be further explored below, but suffice it to say that a study of Jonah merits a careful consideration of its context and intended message to the original audience.

Nineveh – That Great City

The city of Nineveh is central to the book of Jonah since it was the target of Jonah's preaching mission, and for that reason some background on the city is helpful for context. The name Nineveh comes from the word Nina or Ninuwa,

---

[8] Mark J. Boda and J. Gordon McConville, 456.

[9] Loken, Israel P., *The Old Testament Prophetic Books: An Introduction*, Xulon Press (2010), p. 64.

which itself appears in ancient cuneiform texts and the cuneiform symbol for the word was comprised of a fish in an enclosure:

> The *Ninua* of cuneiform sources goes back to an earlier form, *Ninuwa,* which would seem to underlie the received biblical writing. In addition to the syllabic spelling, the cuneiform texts also occasionally use a pseudologographic form, *Nina,* which is the combination of two signs (AB + HA) that represent an enclosure with a fish inside. This reading is of particular interest in light of the prophet Jonah being swallowed by a large fish (Jon. 1:17).[10]

DeVries further noted that "[t]he cuneiform symbols, or ideograms, indicate that the name was associated with not only the fish, but also Nina, the river goddess...."[11] According to Old Testament scholar Eugene Merrill, the name means "fishtown" and the Ninevites believed their city was created by a fish god.[12] The Ninevites worshiped, among others, the fish-man god Dagon, usually illustrated with both human and fish features.

Nineveh was founded by Nimrod (Genesis 10:11) and became a major cultural center in the third millennium BC. At that time, it was a province of the Akkadian Empire and housed a temple for Ishtar, the pagan goddess of love and war.

---

[10] Paul J. Achtemeier, Harper & Row and Society of Biblical Literature, *Harper's Bible Dictionary* (San Francisco: Harper & Row, 1985), 707.

[11] DeVries, LaMoine F., *Cities of the Biblical World*, Hendrickson Publishers, Inc. (1997), p. 60.

[12] Smith and Page, p. 246.

Though it was under Babylonian control for some time, it later regained its independence, and during the 14th, 13th and 12th centuries BC, Nineveh was the site of extensive building programs by Assyrian kings, especially Shalmaneser I (1274-1245 BC) and Tiglath Pileser I (1115-1071 BC). During the 9th, 8th, and 7th centuries, the Assyrian Empire became strong and attacked nations to the east, north, and west, including Israel. Shalmaneser III (859-824 BC) made Nineveh his base for military operations. Ashurnasirpal II (883-859 BC) and Sargon II (722-705 BC) constructed palaces in Nineveh.

At the time that Jonah announced God's message to Nineveh, the city was protected by two walls. The strength of an ancient city was typically measured by the size of its wall, and the inner wall of Nineveh was 50 feet wide and 100 feet high. The circumference of the city was less than 8 miles (less than a 2-mile diameter), but the metro area included additional smaller cities that were probably considered part of Nineveh (see Genesis 10:11-12). The IVP Dictionary explained:

> At the time of the greatest prosperity of Nineveh as described by Jonah, the city was surrounded by a circuit wall almost 13 kilometers (eight miles) long. This "great city" (Jon. 1:2) would have had an area sufficient to contain a population of 120,000, as indicated by Jonah 4:11 and 3:2. Evidence for this is provided by Calah to the south, where 69,754 persons lived in a city half the size of Nineveh. As a result, it would have required a "three day's journey" to go around the city, and a "day's journey" would have been needed to reach the city center from the outlying

suburbs, just as the Book of Jonah reports
(Jon. 3:4).[13]

Before Jonah's arrival, two plagues struck Nineveh (in 765
and 759 BC) and a total eclipse of the sun occurred on June
15, 763 BC. Also, in the first half of the eighth century B.C.,
especially between the death of Adad-nirari III (810–783
B.C.) and the reign of Tiglath-Pileser III (745–727 B.C.),
Assyria was fighting to defend itself against the Arameans
and Urartians. Due to these events, some scholars suggest
that the Ninevites were ripe for repentance when Jonah
arrived in or about 759 BC.

Nineveh reached its point of greatest strength during the
end of the 8th and beginning of the 7th centuries with
renewed building programs (some 50 years after Jonah's
arrival in the city). In 731 BC, King Ahaz of Judah (732- 715
BC) became a vassal of Tiglath-Pileser III. Tiglath-Pileser
reestablished Assyrian supremacy, annexing the Aramean
kingdoms and subjugating Israel and Judah (cf. 2 Kgs 15–
16).[14] Tiglath-Pileser's successor, Shalmaneser V (727-722
BC) attacked Samaria and finally defeated it in 722 BC (2
Kings 17:3-6; 18:9-10).   Shalmaneser V died that year,
though, and his successor, Sargon II (722-705 BC), finished
the job. Some 21 years later, in 701 BC, Sargon's successor,
Sennacherib (705-681 BC), invaded Judah and destroyed 46
towns, but could not take Jerusalem. His invasion force of
185,000 soldiers surrounded Jerusalem for an attack, but

---

[13] Ronald F. Youngblood, F. F. Bruce, and R. K. Harrison, Thomas Nelson
Publishers, eds., *Nelson's New Illustrated Bible Dictionary* (Nashville, TN:
Thomas Nelson, Inc., 1995).

[14] Billy K. Smith and Franklin S. Page, *Amos, Obadiah, Jonah*, vol. 19B, The New
American Commentary (Nashville: Broadman & Holman Publishers, 1995), 204-
205.

according to the Biblical record was destroyed in a single night (2 Kings 18:17-18; 19:32-36; Isaiah 37:36), after which Sennacherib returned to Nineveh. Sennacherib's own annals placed a more positive spin on his defeat:

> As to Hezekiah, the Jew, he did not submit to my yoke. I laid siege to 46 of his strong cities, walled forts and to the countless small villages in their vicinity, and conquered (them) by means of well-stamped (earth-)ramps, and battering-rams brought (thus) near to the walls (combined with) the attack by foot soldiers, (using) mines, breeches as well as sapper work. I drove out (of them) 200,150 people, young and old, male and female, horses, mules, donkeys, camels, big and small cattle beyond counting and considered (them) booty.[15]

Sennacherib built a new palace at Nineveh and made it the capital of the Assyrian Empire. Shortly thereafter, however, the Assyrian Empire declined, and ultimately, Nineveh fell to the Babylonians, Medes, and Scythians in August, 612 BC, a judgment God announced ahead of time through the prophet Nahum.

In more recent history, portions of Nineveh were excavated. C. J. Rich originally investigated the site in 1820. Paul Botta directed a limited excavation in 1842, followed by more extensive excavations in the latter half of the 1800's sponsored by the British Museum and directed by Henry Layard, H. Rassam, George Smith, and W. Budge. Their

---

[15] Patterson, Richard D., *Nahum, Habakkuk, Zephaniah*, Biblical Studies Press (2003), p. 60.

findings included palaces, artwork and sculptures, and an extensive library. Additional excavations were performed by R. C. Thompson from 1927 – 1932. The IVP Dictionary generally describes the grandeur of the ancient Nineveh that has been recovered:

> The remains of Nineveh are hidden in two mounds on either bank of the Hawsar River. One is Kouyunjik Tepe, where the palaces of Esarhaddon and Ashurbanipal were discovered, and the other, on the south bank, is Nebi Younis (the Prophet Jonah), where the palace of Sennacherib stood. These palaces were unusually large, built upon raised platforms about 75 feet high. At the gates of the palaces stood winged lions with human faces. The walls were lined with alabaster and other beautiful stones. On the walls were reliefs depicting the military campaigns of the kings of Assyria and their hunting expeditions, plus mythological and other scenes. Sennacherib's palace occupied the southeastern quarter of the city. It was here that the relief portraying the siege and conquest of Lachish was discovered. The city wall was more than 3 miles long and according to the king's description it had no less than 15 gates. Sennacherib encircled the inner wall with an outer one which, in his words, 'was high like a mountain'. The whole city was surrounded by gardens full of scented plants and irrigated by channels that drew water from the neighboring rivers. The great library of Ashurbanipal, containing 25,000 clay

tablets dealing with historical, literary and religious matters, was found in Kouyunjik.[16]

The ruins are on the east side of the Tigris River opposite modern day Mosul, Iraq, some 220 miles from Baghdad. Excavations at the smaller mound (Tell Nebi Yuns—"the mound of the prophet Jonah") have been limited since it is the location of an Islamic mosque dedicated to Jonah.

The People of Nineveh

Dr. Elliott Johnson, in his commentary on Nahum, wrote: "Ninevah was the capital of one of the cruelest, vilest, most powerful, and most idolatrous empires in the world....Gross idolatry was practiced in Ninevah and throughout the Assyrian Empire. The religion of Assyria was Babylonian in origin but in Assyria the national god was Assur, whose high priest and representative was the king."[17] We see the notorious Assyrian cruelty reflected in the writings of Assyria's kings. For instance, Ashurnasirpal II (883-859 BC) boasted of his military victories:

> I stormed the mountain peaks and took them. In the midst of the mighty mountain I slaughtered them; with their blood I dyed the mountain red like wool.... The heads of their warriors I cut off, and I formed them into a pillar over against their city; their young men and maidens I burned in the fire.
>
> I took the city, and 800 of their fighting men

---

[16] Avraham Negev, *The Archaeological Encyclopedia of the Holy Land* (New York: Prentice Hall Press, 1990).
[17] Walvoord and Zuck, pp. 1493-94.

I put to the sword, and cut off their heads. Multitudes I captured alive, and the rest of them I burned with fire, and carried off their heavy spoil. I formed a pillar of the living and of heads over against their city gate, and 700 men I impaled on stakes over against their city gate. The city I destroyed, I devastated, and turned it into a mound and ruin heap. Their young men and their maidens I burned in the fire.

As to one of the leaders he captured, "I flayed [him], his skin I spread upon the wall of the city...." The next king, Shalmaneser III (859-824 BC), similarly wrote of his military victories: "A pyramid of heads I reared in front of his city. Their youths and their maidens I burnt up in the flames." And similarly:

Like Adad I [Shalmaneser III] rained destruction upon them. With their blood I dyed [the mountain] like red wool ... His cities I turned to wastes. Arzashku, together with the cities of its neighborhood, I destroyed, I devastated, [I burned with fire]. Four pyramids of heads I erected in front of its gate. Some (of his people) I fastened alive into these pyramids, others I hung up on stakes around the pyramids.

And Sennacherib (705-681 BC) wrote of his enemies: "I cut their throats like lambs. I cut off their precious lives [as one cuts] a string. Like the many waters of a storm I made [the contents of] their gullets and entrails run down upon the wide earth....Their hands I cut off." Still later, Ashurbanipal (669-626 BC) wrote of how he treated a captured leader from one of his conquests: "I pierced his chin with my keen hand dagger. Through his jaw... I passed a rope, put a dog chain upon him and made him occupy... a kennel." Ashurbanipal fought Egypt and had his officials hang the Egyptian bodies "on stakes [and] stripped off their skins and covered the city walls with them." Quite appropriately, the prophet Nahum, moved by the Holy Spirit, called Nineveh "the city of blood" (Nahum 3:1) and a cruel city (Nahum 3:19).

Ashurbanipal attributed his military prowess to himself and his pagan gods: "I [am] Ashurbanipal, the great [king], the mighty king, king of the universe, king of Assyria ... The great gods ... magnified my name; they made my rule powerful." Esarhaddon (681-669 BC) likewise wrote: "I am powerful, I am all powerful, I am a hero, I am gigantic, I am colossal, I am honored, I am magnified, I am without equal among all kings, the chosen one of Asshur, Nabu, and Marduk." The words of these kings bring to mind God's Word through Obadiah the prophet aimed at a similarly arrogant Edom: "The pride of thine heart hath deceived thee, thou that dwellest in the clefts of the rock, whose habitation is high; that saith in his heart, Who shall bring me down to the ground?" (Obadiah 3). God brought down Nineveh in 612 BC.

The Man, Jonah

The Pharisees in John's gospel rebuked Nicodemus for suggesting that they follow their law in their treatment of Jesus: "Art thou also of Galilee? Search and look: for out of Galilee ariseth no prophet." (John 7:52) But prophets did arise from Galilee, including Jonah, who was a prophet from

Gath-hepher, a short distance north of Nazareth. (2 Kings 14:25) The name Jonah means "dove." His father was Ammitai, a name that means "my true one." Jonah was a prophet during the reign of Jeroboam II (793-753 BC). Jeroboam II was not a godly king, but was probably Israel's (i.e., the Northern Kingdom's) most powerful king politically. Under his reign, as prophesied by Jonah and recorded in 2 Kings 14, the boundaries of Israel were extended "to approximately their extent in Solomon's time (excluding of course the Southern Kingdom's territory belonging to Judah and Benjamin)."[18] Conservative scholars tend to place Jonah's preaching to Nineveh around 759 BC during the reign of the Assyrian king Ashur-dan III (772-754 BC).[19] Beyond these scant details, we only know of Jonah what we learn from his experiences that are recorded there.

Author

The Book of Jonah contains no explicit reference to an author or to a chronological setting. The book does not claim authorship by Jonah, nor does it contain use of the first-person singular. There is also no statement elsewhere in Scripture that can be used to determine the author. In fact, if it were not for 2 Kings 14:25, we would know almost nothing about the historical situation or the prophet. Therefore, it is impossible to know for certain whether the book is *by* Jonah or only *about* him. While most scholars doubt authorship by Jonah, some affirm his contribution, at least in supplying information.[20] The most that can be said

---

[18] Walvoord and Zuck, p. 566.

[19] Walvoord and Zuck, p. 1462.

[20] Billy K. Smith and Franklin S. Page, *Amos, Obadiah, Jonah*, vol. 19B, The New American Commentary (Nashville: Broadman & Holman Publishers, 1995), 205-206.

with certainty is that since Jonah was a prophet of the Lord
(2 Kgs 14:25), and following the lead of other prophets, he
could have written this book.[21]

Historicity

"Scholars have labored to categorize the book and have
debated its historicity. Though many regard the book as a
parable or allegory, the traditional view understands it as a
historically accurate account of Jonah's experiences, albeit
one with a theological purpose."[22] The three more common
positions are either to affirm the historicity of the book in
total, to deny it altogether, or to view the book either as an
allegory or parable. Within Judaism and Christianity, the
book was historically assumed to be an accurate historical
account, but the growing trend in the past two centuries has
been to understand the book as a parable written several
centuries after Jonah's death. As Chisholm explained: "The
book's historicity has been questioned for several reasons.
The primary barrier relates to the miraculous events it
records, especially Jonah's being swallowed alive by the great
fish, in which he survived (and even prayed!) for three days
before being spit up on the shore."[23] Indeed, "[b]ecause of
these [miraculous] events the book's historicity has been
called into question and the prophecy variously viewed as
mythological, symbolical, fictional, allegorical, and as a
poetic parable much like Isaiah's parable of the vineyard
(Isa. 5) or the parable of the good Samaritan."[24] In fact,

---

[21] Billy K. Smith and Franklin S. Page, *Amos, Obadiah, Jonah*, vol. 19B, The New
American Commentary (Nashville: Broadman & Holman Publishers, 1995), 206.

[22] Chisholm, Robert B., Jr., p. 119.

[23] Chisholm, Robert R., Jr., pp. 119-120.

[24] Freeman, Hobart E., *An Introduction to the Old Testament Prophets*, Faith
Ministries & Publications (2004), p. 160.

critics have questioned the historicity of Jonah due to its inclusion of the supernatural, skepticism concerning the supposed repentance of the people of Nineveh, the allegedly fallacious reference to the "king of Nineveh" (Jonah 3:6), and other issues.

One of the older commentaries on Jonah placed the question of historicity into perspective:

> The miraculous element in the book has led many critics to doubt its historical character, and to consider it as romance, allegory, or parable. The miracles, they say, are so prodigious, so wanting in sufficient motive, as to be utterly incredible, and to prove that the writer manifestly intends his work to be regarded as a fiction with a didactic purpose, like some of those writings which are preserved in our Apocrypha. Others see in it only a dream; others, again, regard it as a Jewish adaptation of a Greek or Babylonian myth; others explain away the supernatural portion of the story, as *e.g.* that Jonah was saved by a vessel which was called, or bore as its emblem, a sea-monster. Against all these suggestions we must place the fact that the work comes before us as history; and we need very strong arguments to dislodge us from this position. Such, however, are not produced; and we should have heard nothing of them were it not for the unbelief in the supernatural which underlies all such criticism, or a tendency to reject, *primâ facie*, all narratives which do not meet the standard

of evidence which modern critics set up and worship. Of course, there is in itself nothing repugnant to reverence in considering the book as an inspired allegory intended to set forth certain great spiritual truths, as, for instance, the temporary death of the Jewish nation and its resurrection anew to a national existence (Wright, 'Biblical Essays,' p. 70); but does the work confirm such view? We think not.[25]

Unsurprisingly, Jonah has become somewhat of a litmus test for how a person views the entire Bible. This author accepts the traditional, conservative view that upholds the complete historicity of the book. Indeed, those affirming the historicity of Jonah have the high ground: "It is important to note that there is ample evidence to support the historicity of the book, and surprisingly little to undermine it."[26]

That said, we should briefly respond to the major attacks on the historicity of the book. As already indicated above, questioning the historicity of Jonah because it contains supernatural elements argues too much. Such skepticism attacks the veracity of the entire Bible. Moreover, such skepticism is exactly that and no more. Standing on the hill of denial neither constitutes a historically founded argument nor evidence. It is merely to state a position, and so does not move the needle in weighing the quantum of historical data. Turning to the possibility that the people of Nineveh repented during Jonah's ministry, we must note that in the

---

[25] H. D. M. Spence-Jones, ed., *Jonah*, The Pulpit Commentary (London; New York: Funk & Wagnalls Company, 1909), ix.

[26] Mark J. Boda and J. Gordon McConville, 460.

context of Assyrian history, the time was exactly right for Jonah's message and the Ninevites' response:

> As to the improbability of the general repentance in Nineveh described in Jonah 3, this must now be tempered by the recognition that our historical evidence preserves the fact that things were not going well for the Ninevites at approximately the time Jonah served as a prophet (toward the end of the first half of the eight century BC). Military and diplomatic losses internationally were coupled with famine and popular uprisings domestically during the time of Ashur-dan III (773-756 BC), the king most likely to be the monarch described in Jonah 3. In addition, both an earthquake and an eclipse, dreaded major omens to the highly superstitious Assyrians, were experienced concurrently to other problems occurring at that time. A weak monarch reeling from domestic and international turmoil could well have welcomed the chance to solidify his acceptance among a suspicious populace, already set on edge by the prevailing problems, via the sort of royal proclamation preserved in Jonah 3:7-9.[27]

It is frequently argued that Jonah was wrong on the historical facts, and especially in his reference to the "king of Nineveh," which point requires us to consider both the historical data for the ancient usage of the title "king" and the status of Nineveh within the Assyrian Empire at the time of Jonah:

---

[27] Mark J. Boda and J. Gordon McConville, 460.

The idea that Nineveh could not have had a "king" is a problem often raised against the historical accuracy of the book. The assumption that the phrase "king of Nineveh"...in Jonah 3:6 reflects both a lack of understanding of the Assyrian Empire (so that it is analogous to speaking of "the king of London"...) and a befuddled historical memory (since Nineveh could not have been the capital of Assyria in Jonah's time, according to the Assyrian records themselves) has been a central objection to the book's historicity. The reply to this objection requires an appreciation of two facts: (1) "king of Nineveh" is a simple, comprehensible phrase in the context of the book; (2) it is entirely possible that an Assyrian king would be present in Nineveh early in the eighth century BC whether or not Nineveh was technically the capital...of the Assyrian Empire.[28]

To the first issue, it may be answered that it was common in the ancient world for a king to be identified with a designation relative to one city. For instance, Sihon is referenced both as "king of the Amorites" who lived in Heshbon and "king of Heshbon." (Deuteronomy 1:4, 3:2, 4:46 versus Deuteronomy 2:24, 26, 30) Similarly, Jabin is "king of Canaan" and "king of Hazor." (Judges 4:2, 23, 24 versus Judges 4:17) Thus, "a king could be associated with a capital or main city within his empire, as well as with the empire itself (see, e.g., 2 Sam. 8;5; 1 Kings 11:23 where

[28] Mark J. Boda and J. Gordon McConville, 460.

Hadadezer's kingship is associated with 'Zobah' even though his control extended considerably further)."[29] Thus, Israel's King Ahab is referred to as the "king of Samaria" in 1 Kings 21:1.

Turning then to the question of whether the king of Assyria would have ever been called the king of Nineveh, as opposed to the king of some other town in the Empire, the argument is usually made that Nineveh did not become the actual capital of the Assyrian Empire except in the time of Sennacherib (705-682 BC). This assertion is questionable, but even if true, it is not necessary to establish that Nineveh was the capital of Assyria to vindicate Jonah's reference to the king of Nineveh:

> Nineveh may well have been at least an alternate capital, if not the capital of Assyria throughout much of the first half of the eighth century BC. We know, for example, that Shalmaneser I (1275-1246 BC) began an expansion of the city, and that by the time of Tiglath-Pileser I (1114-1076 BC), Nineveh had become an alternative royal residence to both Ashur and Calah. Thereafter, a palace of some sort appears to have been established in the city and used by various kings, including Ashurnasirpal II (883-859 BC) before Jonah's time, and Sargon II (722-705 BC) after Jonah's time. It therefore is likely that Nineveh functioned as a royal residence, even if not the capital technically, during most of the eighth century BC... Our knowledge of the affairs of the weak kings of Assyria between

---

[29] Mark J. Boda and J. Gordon McConville, 460.

the latter years of Adad-nirari III (811-784 BC) and Tiglath Pileser III (745-728 BC) is spotty. It is probable, however, that each of these kings (Shalmaneser IV [783-774 BC], Ashur-dan III [773-756 BC] and Ashur-nirari V [755-746 BC]) ruled at least part of the time from Nineveh. Ashur-dan III shifted his residence at least once, and possibly more. Thus, regardless of whether the ancient Assyrians thought of capitals in the same way that moderns do, it is clear that Nineveh, because of its size and wealth, became de facto the chief city of the Neo-Assyrian Empire and host to royalty during much of that period. There is therefore nothing in the phrase "king of Nineveh" in Jonah 3:6 that can be falsified historically.[30]

Accepting the historicity of the book, however, does not settle the questions of genre and proper interpretation. As Freeman explained, "Conservative Christians have always held to the *literal historicity* of the book, viewing it as an actual account of the experiences of the prophet Jonah in the eighth century B.C. Those who hold the book to be historical also view the prophecy as having *symbolic* and *typical* reference to Israel and Christ."[31] In my view, we can put a finer edge on the genre than just accepting the possibility of symbolic or typical references. What is critical is not merely that the events are historical, but that God assigned Jonah the task of going to Nineveh so that Jonah's actions and the reactions of others (the pagan sailors, the fish, the Ninevites) could be on display as the prophetic

---

[30] Mark J. Boda and J. Gordon McConville, 461.
[31] Freeman, Hobert E., p. 162.

message to the rebellious Israel of Jonah's day. "If the events in the book actually happened, then the audience's existential identification with the characters and circumstances is invariably heightened. People act more surely upon what they believe to be true in fact than upon what they merely consider likely in theory."[32]

Genre of the Book and Interpretive Approach

Although Jonah is widely understood as a parable or allegory, with various symbolic interpretations, the view is not well supported. In the first place, there is no indication in the book that it is to be taken as an allegory or parable. Instead, it begins, "Now the word of the Lord came unto Jonah the son of Amittai, saying ...." Prophecies in the Bible are often introduced in this fashion (see, e.g., Joel 1:1). The Book of Jonah begins just as we would expect a prophetic book to begin. Throughout the book, the details of the story have all the indicia of being an historical account. Notably, the cities referred to are all real places: Nineveh (1:2; 3:2-4, 6-7; 4:11), Tarshish (1:3; 4:2), and Joppa (1:3). Moreover, parables in the Bible do not use real persons as characters, but no one disputes that Jonah was a real historical figure. (2 Kings 14:24-26) Allegories may use real persons' names, but the text tends to be explicit that an allegory is being used. (e.g., allegory in Galatians 4 about Hagar and Sarah; the rock that supplied water to the Israelites in the wilderness was a real rock, but it was also symbolic of Jesus Christ, 1 Corinthians 10:4) The IVP Dictionary summarized the case against viewing Jonah as an allegory or parable:

---

[32] Mark J. Boda and J. Gordon McConville, 460.

As sensational, didactic, prophetic narrative, the book shares features with those genres of literature known as parable and allegory, but it is neither of these. Parables are brief (not four chapters long), normally containing a single scene or two, make comparison to people or things outside the story who are the real focus, and end with a punch line that draws the hearer up short as it teaches a lesson, the reader hopefully seeing a personally relevant truth in the story. And parables have anonymous figures as their characters. The book of Jonah borders on some of these characteristics but manifests none of them exactly. Moreover, parables are obviously fictional. That is, they are illustrative narrative rather than historical narrative. Jonah is by no means obviously fictional.

Nor is Jonah an allegory. An allegory is an extended analogy, sometimes including extended metaphors, in which the meaning of the story is found in concepts and actions outside the story to which the story points analogically. It would be an unusual allegory indeed that waited to the end (the fourth chapter in the case of Jonah) to reveal the point of its hero's actions. Allegories are distinctly constructed so as to point beyond themselves at each stage. The figures in an allegory are patently symbolic and fictional, and the audience must realize this at once if the allegory is to be effective. Jonah does not fit this pattern either.[33]

Most importantly, Jesus referred to Jonah as an historical figure in Matthew 12:38-42 and 16:4 and Luke 11:32. Those holding the view that the book is a parable argue that Jesus' reference to Jonah does not mean that the events in the book actually occurred, but either (i) that Jesus was simply not going to disavow his audience of their false understanding or (ii) that Jesus used the reference without explanation because the parable was well known. In like fashion, I might refer to someone as an Ebenezer Scrooge without believing in the historicity of this fictional character. The flaw in this argument is that in the Matthew 12 passage, Jesus refers to the Ninevites that repented rising up in the future in judgment against the Jewish generation of Jesus' day, then in parallel fashion, refers to the queen of the south (Sheba who visited Solomon, indisputably a reference to a historical figure) doing the same. By this comparison, Jesus affirms his understanding that the Ninevites and the queen are real persons. And in any event, fictitious characters in parables do not rise up in judgment. Jesus plainly asserted the historicity of the book, and to suggest that Jesus was only accommodating his audience's false beliefs about the book is to have Jesus not only winking at error, but promoting it.

We may conclude, then, that Jonah is historical, but it is more than that—it is also indisputably a narrative with a prophetic purpose. "All biblical narratives are didactic to one degree or another, but in the case of Jonah the narrator has carefully shaped the story for an obviously didactic purpose... the book of Jonah may be described not simply as

---

[33] Mark J. Boda and J. Gordon McConville, 458.

a prophetic narrative, but as a didactic prophetic narrative."[34] The position taken in this commentary is that the events in Jonah actually happened, but more than that, Jonah's mission was intended by God as an object lesson for the original audience, Israel, to whom God was making yet another appeal for repentance.

Jonah was a representative for Israel. His disobedience to God's direction pictured their flagrant rebellion. Jonah's deliverance by fish and second chance to go to Nineveh put on display God's longsuffering and mercy, as does God's treatment toward the people of Nineveh. Every aspect of the story, from sailors to fish to Nineveh to the gourd of chapter 4 and the critical dialogue in chapter 4 about Jonah's anger, was purposed to convict Israel and call the nation to repentance. What God did through Amos and Hosea largely (but not exclusively) by their messages, God did through the events in Jonah as a divine object lesson, and in this sense the book is a didactic prophetic narrative. Ultimately, the pagan sailors and the pagan Ninevites responded favorably to the light God gave them, while Jonah never obeyed in faith. To the end, Jonah wanted the Ninevites to die and rebuked God for showing mercy to them. Jonah's behavior, to put it lightly, was embarrassing and repugnant against the background of the sailors and people of Nineveh, who with minimal revelation, responded obediently. Jonah, and the nation Israel, had substantial revelation from God, but refused to obey.

There is substantial precedent for God not merely speaking through prophets in word, but also in acts with symbolic significance. For instance, God assigned the prophet Hosea the task of marrying a woman God warned him would

---

[34] Mark J. Boda and J. Gordon McConville, 458.

subsequently be unfaithful. (Hosea 1:2) The text records that Hosea obeyed God by marrying a woman named Gomer, who subsequently bore him children and was unfaithful. The actions of Hosea and Gomer, and even the names of their children, were rich with prophetic significance to the Israel of Hosea's (and Jonah's) day. In particular, Gomer's unfaithfulness pictured Israel's idolatry. In this way, it was not Hosea's words, but his actions and those of Gomer that provided a divine object lesson to Israel. God similarly assigned symbolic acts to Ezekiel, four of which are included in Ezekiel 4-5, as summarized by Loken:

> First, the prophet is told to take a soft clay tablet and inscribe on it a picture of Jerusalem. Ezekiel is then directed to lay siege against it using siege walls, ramps and battering rams. This symbolic act was designed to show that the city of Jerusalem was about to come under siege. Second, the prophet is commanded to lie on his side for a total of 430 days; 390 days to represent the sins of Israel and 40 days to represent the sins of Judah. This symbolic act was intended to demonstrate the length of the nation's apostasy, each day representing a year (4:5)....
> Third, the prophet is instructed to purchase food and cook it using dung as fuel. The amount of food and water Ezekiel is commanded to consume had to be carefully measured out. This symbolic act was designed to portray the horrific conditions that the inhabitants of Jerusalem would have to endure during the siege. Fourth, the prophet is ordered to shave his head and divide the

hair into three parts using a scale. A third was to be burned, and third was to be struck with a sword, and a third was to be scattered by the wind. This symbolic act was intended to reveal the three fates that awaited the inhabitants of Jerusalem. Some would die by famine, some would die by the sword, and some would be scattered among the nations.[35]

Jonah was assigned the task of going to preach to Nineveh, and while his message to Nineveh was a typical prophetic message—God speaking through the words of a prophet—his message to Israel was on par of what we find in Hosea 1 and Ezekiel 4-5 and 12. In every case, the actions were real and were put on display for the intended audience. So also with Jonah's excursion to Nineveh, as Loken explains:

The book of Jonah was written to call the nation of Israel to repentance. Jonah is the first of three writing prophets to the northern kingdom of Israel. The other prophets are Amos and Hosea. Together, these prophets form a threefold attack on Israel. All three prophets have the same message; the nation is about to experience the judgment of God. While this message is plainly recognized in Amos and Hosea, the message in Jonah is more subtle, at least it seems that way to the modern audience. However, rest assured that the original audience of Jonah got the intended message.[36]

[35] Loken, Israel P., pp. 317-18.
[36] Loken, Israel P., p. 65.

Jonah's response to God's command to go to Nineveh, and then the reactions of everyone else including the sailors, Ninevites, fish, plant and worm, formed the message of repentance to Israel. Indeed, everything and everyone responded obediently to God throughout the book with the exception of Jonah as representative of Israel. Jesus confirmed this interpretation in his teaching in Matthew 12. The Pharisees challenged Jesus about his disciples allegedly violating their Sabbath traditions (e.g., Matthew 12:2). Jesus answered them by reference to David eating the showbread in the Tabernacle, then commented: "But I say unto you, That in this place is one greater than the temple..." (Matthew 12:6) Later in the chapter, after the Pharisees decided to murder Jesus (Matthew 12:14), he casted out a demon. Rather than acknowledging the Messianic nature of Jesus' miracle and believing, the Pharisees accused Jesus of doing the miracle "by Beelzebub the prince of the devils." (Matthew 12:24) Jesus rebuked them and then they demanded another sign. (Matthew 12:38) To this demand, Jesus offered the following:

> Matthew 12:39 But he answered and said unto them, An evil and adulterous generation seeketh after a sign; and there shall no sign be given to it, but the sign of the prophet Jonas: 40 For as Jonas was three days and three nights in the whale's belly; so shall the Son of man be three days and three nights in the heart of the earth. 41 The men of Nineveh shall rise in judgment with this generation, and shall condemn it: because they repented at the preaching of Jonas; and, behold, a greater than Jonas *is* here. 42 The queen of the south shall rise up in the judgment with this generation, and shall condemn it: for she

came from the uttermost parts of the earth to
hear the wisdom of Solomon; and, behold, a
greater than Solomon *is* here.

Jesus' point, with his reference to Jonah and to the queen of
Sheba, related to how people respond to God's revelation.
The gentile "queen of the south" traveled a great distance to
hear Solomon's wisdom, yet the Pharisees rejected the
words of Jesus, "a greater than Solomon." Similarly, the
pagan "men of Nineveh" responded to Jonah's brief message
while the Pharisees rejected the revelation of God through
His Son Jesus. Because of this rejection of the greater
revelation in Jesus Christ, the "men of Nineveh" who
responded to far less revelation "shall rise in judgment with
this generation, and shall condemn it." The principle Jesus
applied in the first century to that generation of Israel is the
same principle underlying Jonah's message to his
generation—the response of the men of Nineveh to God's
message should convict Israel of their rejection of God's
message.

We should further observe both that Jesus affirmed the
historicity of Jonah and that the message of Jonah fails if it
is not historical. In other words, if the generation of Israel
living during Jesus' earthly ministry rejected the historicity
of Jonah preaching to Nineveh and Nineveh repenting, then
Jesus' message about the men of Nineveh rising in judgment
would have no power of persuasion. It is only because the
people of Nineveh underline actually repented at Jonah's teaching that
the divine object lesson had any force, in Jonah's day, during
Jesus's earthly ministry, and today. To reject the historicity
of Jonah is to remove the foundation of the message and
render it a nullity. Of the connection between the application
of the message of Jonah in his day and during Jesus' earthly
ministry, Loken observed:

Jonah himself represents Israel (the dove was the symbol of Israel) in the story and is a sign to the nation of her disobedience. The prophet is also a sign of judgment on the nation Israel in Matthew 12:39-40. In Jonah's day, the judgment of Israel came forty years after the prophet's message; in Christ's day, the judgment of Israel came forty years after His declaration. It is likely that the prophet's message "Yet forty days and Nineveh will be overthrown" (3:4) is to be understood "Yet forty years and Israel will be overthrown."[37]

Finally, a brief comment about the relationship between the three writing prophets to Israel is in order as that relationship supports the core interpretation of Jonah offered in this commentary. Again, Loken summarized this relationship:

The relationship between these three books is routinely overlooked by modern interpreters even though the similarities between the books are striking. All three books are written to the northern kingdom of Israel. All three prophets minister during the reign of Jeroboam II. All three prophets are instructed to "go" (Heb. *Halak*; Hos. 1:2; 3:1; Amos 7:15; Jon. 1:2; 3:2) and perform a specific task given them by the Lord. All three prophets emphasize the Hebrew word *shub* (often translated "return"), a term that is used in all three books to describe repentance (e.g., Hos. 3:5; 5:4; 6:1; 7:10, 16; 11:5; 12:6; 14:1, 2;

---

[37] Loken, Israel P., p. 66.

Amos 4:6, 8, 9, 10, 11; Jon. 3:8, 9, 10). All three prophets speak of Israel going to Assyria (Hos. 7:11; 8:9; 9:3; 11:5, 11; Amos 5:27; Jonah, being used figuratively as representative of Israel, travels to Assyria). In Jonah 1:2, the prophet is sent to preach against Nineveh because their "wickedness" (Heb. *Raah*) has come before God's face (Heb. *Panim*). The same words are used in Hosea 7:2 to describe the apostasy of Israel. In Jonah 3:9, 10, the Lord "relents" (Heb. *naham*) concerning the judgment he has prescribed for Nineveh. The same word is used in Amos 7:3, 3 to describe the Lord's change of heart concerning a judgment prescribed for Israel (cf. Hos. 13:14). In Jonah 4:8, the prophet is afflicted by an "east wind"(Heb. *Qadim*). The same word is used in Hosea 13:15 to describe the future judgment of Israel. Finally, and perhaps most significant, Hosea twice characterizes the nation Israel as a *yonah* (i.e., Jonah; Hos. 7:11; 11:11).[38]

Outline and Purpose of Jonah

Purpose: God uses what transpired in the life of the prophet Jonah to help Israel see its own wicked heart and need to turn to God as it sees the positive responses to God's limited revelation from the sailors and the Ninevites in contrast to the rebellious response of Jonah to God's substantial revelation. The looming judgment announced to Nineveh will also befall Israel if they do not repent.

---

[38] Loken, Israel P., pp. 65-66.

1. JONAH'S REBELLIOUS HEART (ch. 1)
   a. God commands Jonah to preach (1:1-2)
   b. Jonah disobeys God and runs (1:3)
   c. God pursues Jonah (1:4)
   d. Pagan sailors fear God (1:5-8)
   e. Jonah talks the talk (1:9)
   f. Jonah would rather die than repent (1:10-12)
   g. Pagan sailors show compassion on Jonah (1:13)
   h. Pagan sailors pray to God (1:14-15)
   i. Pagan sailors sacrifice to God (1:16)
   j. God intervenes for Jonah (1:17)

2. JONAH'S UNREPENTANT HEART (ch. 2)
   a. Jonah prays because of his affliction (2:1-4)
   b. Jonah hits bottom but no repentance (2:5-7)
   c. Jonah talks the talk (2:8)
   d. Jonah makes a vow (2:9)
   e. God intervenes for Jonah (2:10)

3. JONAH'S UNFAITHFUL HEART (ch. 3)
   a. Jonah heralds the destruction of Nineveh (3:1-4)
   b. Every man, woman and beast repents and mourns the evil and violence of Nineveh (3:5-9)
   c. God intervenes for Nineveh (3:10)

4. JONAH'S ANGRY HEART (ch. 4)
   a. Angry Jonah wants to die (4:1-3)
   b. God interrogates Jonah (4:4)
   c. Jonah loves his gourd (4:5-6)
   d. God takes Jonah's gourd (4:7)
   e. Angry Jonah wants to die (4:8)
   f. God intervenes for Jonah (4:9-11)

Chapter 2

Jonah's Rebellious Heart

It has been rightly observed that we tend to have PhD's in picking out the flaws in others but a preschool proficiency in seeing our own. This principle was behind Jesus' question in his famous Sermon on the Mount: "And why beholdest thou the mote that is in thy brother's eye, but considerest not the beam that is in thine own eye?" (Matthew 7:3) We stand as a kitten looking in the mirror and seeing a lion. In the Psalms, David warned against "he [that] flattereth himself in his own eyes" to avoid seeing his flaws. (Psalm 36:2) We make ourselves the heroes in all our stories. The fact is that it can be very difficult to see our own flaws and sins and discern those areas of our lives where we need to let the Holy Spirit do some work. The preacher delivers the message God put on his heart and we assume it is for the person at the other end of the pew. We find it easier to say "amen" than "oh me."

When the words just hit against a brick wall, God may draw us a picture. By way of example, when David committed adultery with Bathsheba and murdered her husband, he failed to acknowledge his sin until God sent the prophet

Nathan to tell him a story about a rich man with many flocks stealing and killing a poor man's "one little ewe lamb, which he had bought and nourished up." (2 Samuel 12:2-3) Upon hearing the story—and, like us, having a PhD in picking out others' flaws—"David's anger was greatly kindled against the man; and he said to Nathan, As the LORD liveth, the man that hath done this thing shall surely die." (2 Samuel 12:5) God had to draw David a picture before he would see and acknowledge the reality of his sinful actions, and then repent of what he had done.

In the Old Testament, God frequently sent prophets to His people to give them His message—often a demand for repentance and turning back to God. They frequently did not heed the message. They saw themselves as being "ok" even though God's prophets kept telling them the truth. Such was the case in Jonah's time, so God drew Israel a picture. The story that begins to unfold in Jonah 1 is God allowing the people of Israel, who desperately needed to see their sin and turn back to God, to do exactly that by seeing it in the life of the prodigal prophet Jonah. Like David, they should have been appalled, but also like David, they needed to realize they were looking at themselves in a mirror and turn back to God before it was too late.

Outline

JONAH'S REBELLIOUS HEART (ch. 1)
- a. God commands Jonah to preach (1:1-2)
- b. Jonah disobeys God and runs (1:3)
- c. God pursues Jonah (1:4)
- d. Pagan sailors fear God (1:5-8)
- e. Jonah talks the talk (1:9)

f. Jonah would rather die than repent (1:10-12)

g. Pagan sailors show compassion on Jonah (1:13)

h. Pagan sailors pray to God (1:14-15)

i. Pagan sailors sacrifice to God (1:16)

j. God intervenes for Jonah (1:17)

Scripture and Comments

Jonah 1:1 Now the word of the LORD came unto Jonah the son of Amittai, saying, 2 Arise, go to Nineveh, that great city, and cry against it; for their wickedness is come up before me. 3 But Jonah rose up to flee unto Tarshish from the presence of the LORD, and went down to Joppa; and he found a ship going to Tarshish: so he paid the fare thereof, and went down into it, to go with them unto Tarshish from the presence of the LORD.

The book starts in typical fashion for a prophetic book, **Now the word of the LORD came unto Jonah**. (e.g., "the word of the Lord came unto Nathan" in 2 Samuel 7:4; "the word of the Lord that came to Micah..." in Micah 1:1) **Jonah** means dove. The name of a prophet usually fits his message. For example, "Nahum" means comfort, and his message of judgment against Nineveh, years after the events recorded in Jonah, was intended to provide comfort to Judah. But in the case of Jonah, we will see that his attitude toward the inhabitants of Nineveh was anything but that of a peaceful dove. Rather, since the dove was a symbol of Israel, Jonah's name was to help the audience (Israel, the Northern Kingdom) identify with him. We are given little biographical information at this point, except that the prophet was **the son of Amittai.** The name **Amittai** means "truthful." The detail we have confirms that **Jonah** was the same prophet that is the subject of 2 Kings 14:25, which refers to "Jonah, the son of Amittai, the prophet, which was of Gathhepher." This tells us he was from Galilee.

Most of the prophetic books follow such an introduction with the content of the message, but that is not the case here. Indeed, whatever message **Jonah** was supposed to **cry against** the **great city** of **Nineveh** is secondary and not revealed here except by implication from God's revelation that **their wickedness is come up before me**. What is at best implied here is revealed in chapter 3. But for now, the focus is on Jonah's response to his calling. God plainly said to Jonah, **Arise, go to Nineveh, that great city, and cry against it; for their wickedness is come up before me**.

The job of a prophet of God is to speak for God. Prophets forth-tell (provide God's word about current events) and foretell (provide God's word about the future). At least in the case of a prophet foretelling a future event, those who hear the prophet's words can know the prophet spoke for God by whether the words come true:

> <u>Deuteronomy 18:20</u> But the prophet, which shall presume to speak a word in my name, which I have not commanded him to speak, or that shall speak in the name of other gods, even that prophet shall die. <u>21</u> And if thou say in thine heart, How shall we know the word which the LORD hath not spoken? <u>22</u> When a prophet speaketh in the name of the LORD, if the thing follow not, nor come to pass, that *is* the thing which the LORD hath not spoken, *but* the prophet hath spoken it presumptuously: thou shalt not be afraid of him.

Obviously, God takes this matter seriously since those who falsely spoke for Him risked a death penalty under the Law. The expectation of the prophet is that he will be God's mouthpiece to faithfully convey to the people the message God has for them.

Accordingly, Jonah's response is shocking. We read in verse 3 that **Jonah rose up to flee unto Tarshish from the presence of the LORD.** We are not even told that Jonah answered God, but simply that he fled God's presence (in Jonah 4 we will learn Jonah did answer). Of course, nothing can excuse his willful disobedience, but we need to understand his calling in light of the historical context of the book outlined in the introductory chapter. The Assyrians were known for their unrestrained brutality, torture and murder, and the proverbial writing was on the wall. These barbaric people were a clear and present danger to Israel. God said that **their wickedness is come up before** Him. Though neither God nor **Jonah** identified **their wickedness**, the king of **Nineveh** later acknowledged their sin of violence. Whereas the events in **Jonah** took place around 759 BC and the prophecy of Nahum is probably dated between 663 and 654 BC, Nahum identified the **wickedness** of the Ninevites that had drawn God's wrath, and those sins were assuredly the same that existed in Jonah's time: idolatry (Nahum 1:14), brutality (2:1), lies and robbery (3:1) and taking captives or slaves (3:1).[1] God spoke against **Nineveh** through Nahum:

> Nahum 3:4 Because of the multitude of the whoredoms of the wellfavoured harlot, the mistress of witchcrafts, that selleth nations through her whoredoms, and families through

---

[1] Walvoord, John F. and Zuck, Roy B., *The Bible Knowledge Commentary, Old Testament*, ChariotVictor Publishing (1985), p. 1496.

her witchcrafts. 5 Behold, I *am* against thee, saith the LORD of hosts; and I will discover thy skirts upon thy face, and I will shew the nations thy nakedness, and the kingdoms thy shame.

God could have simply destroyed **Nineveh**; the fact, as will be revealed in chapter 3, that He would first send **Jonah** with a warning before the destruction, tells us that God was giving **Nineveh** an opportunity to repent and turn from **their wickedness**. From Jonah's perspective, Israel could rest easier with **Nineveh** out of the way. Jonah did not want them to repent and turn from **their wickedness**. From a fleshly standpoint, **Jonah** had good reason to fear the possibility of God showing mercy to **Nineveh**. Knowing how violent the Assyrians were, we need to avoid too quickly looking down our noses at **Jonah**. We can understand (without condoning) why **Jonah** refused to **go to Nineveh** as God commanded, but why did he **flee unto Tarshish**? To answer that question, which really is an anthropological question about how we respond to sin, it is helpful to turn back to the beginning.

In the event of Genesis 3 that we refer to as the Fall, sin first entered the human experience. God provided the first couple an abundant bounty but withheld one tree from them. Satan deceived Eve into believing God was holding back His best (his methods have not changed), and in turn Adam knowingly chose to follow Eve's lead in flagrant disobedience to God's command. See what Moses wrote of the first couple's reaction to sin:

> Genesis 3:6 And when the woman saw that the tree *was* good for food, and that it *was* pleasant to the eyes, and a tree to be desired

to make *one* wise, she took of the fruit thereof, and did eat, and gave also unto her husband with her; and he did eat. 7 And the eyes of them both were opened, and they knew that they *were* naked; and they sewed fig leaves together, and made themselves aprons. 8 And they heard the voice of the LORD God walking in the garden in the cool of the day: and Adam and his wife hid themselves from the presence of the LORD God amongst the trees of the garden.

Note their futile effort to cover their nakedness with fig leaves (people still do this), which nakedness they perceived differently than before because sin immediately affected their perception of reality. Then they heard God walking in the garden and like Jonah they fled to "hid[e] themselves from the presence of the LORD God amongst the trees of the garden." Their response is both heartbreaking and absurd. Adam and Eve desperately hid themselves from God. When God interrogated Adam as to why he ran and hid, Adam said, "I heard thy voice in the garden, and I was afraid, because I was naked; and I hid myself." (Genesis 3:10)

As with our father Adam, it is within our flesh to flee God when we sin. The spiritual response to our personal sin is to run to (not from) God, falling on our knees in confession and repentance. (1 John 1:9) But the flesh whispers to us, "run away." Thus we read verses like Leviticus 26:17: "And I will set my face against you, and ye shall be slain before your enemies: they that hate you shall reign over you; and ye shall flee when none pursueth you." When Israel would turn away from God, a physical result would be that they would lose to their enemies. But more devastating than that, their security in God would be replaced with fear so that they would "flee when none pursueth." Is that not what Adam did? Read the wisdom of God on fleeing: "The wicked flee when no man pursueth: but the righteous are bold as a lion." (Proverbs 28:1) They do not know from what or whom they run, and they can run in different ways because the guilt they are fleeing is within them. It is the ravages of sin. It is seeking fig leaves and not God. One runs to the bottom of a liquor bottle, another to numbing sensual pleasures, another to denial, or to the accumulation of material goods, or to any thing that will provide a moment's peace no matter the cost. Sin produces fear and fleeing from God. In contrast, the righteous before God are bold; they do not run.

We might say of anyone, even a believer, who refuses to deal with their personal sin once it becomes apparent to them, that they are a runner, just like the prophet Jonah and just like the prodigal of Luke 15:11 ff. If we refuse to fall before the God of the universe and plea for forgiveness on the basis of the blood of Jesus Christ, then we are runners. **Jonah** provides a great negative example. We might have expected verse 3 to explain that **Jonah** made the 500-mile trip to **Nineveh**, but instead we are told that **Jonah** ran the opposite direction to **Joppa** to catch a ship to **Tarshish**. The town of **Joppa** was on the Mediterranean coast northwest of Jerusalem. **Joppa** is current day Joffa, and is located about 30 miles south of Caesarea. "According to the Greek historian, Herodotus, Tarshish was Tartessus in southern Spain."[2] This means that the journey to **Tarshish** was a trip some 2,000 miles in the wrong direction. Jonah of all people should have known that you cannot run from an omnipresent God, the creator of the sea and land (1:9).

---

[2] Feinberg, Charles L., *The Minor Prophets*, Moody Publishers (1976), p. 135.

When Jonah arrived at **Joppa**, a **ship** was available **going to Tarshish** and he was able to pay **the fare** and board the vessel. There is a simple lesson here—you cannot determine God's will based simply on the circumstances. There is sometimes confusion among Christians about the issue of decision-making within the will of God. For some, if a desirable opportunity is available, it is assumed to be God's will to take the opportunity. Here is **Jonah** fleeing God, yet he was still able to purchase a **fare** on a ship headed to Spain. To sound pious, **Jonah** might have said God opened a door for him to go to Spain. Christians frequently speak of open and closed doors, yet in the Bible doors are almost always literal doors, and where they are used in the context of an opportunity made available by God, it is for a ministry purpose. (e.g., Acts 14:27) God did open a door—to Nineveh. He did not open a door to Spain, but rather, **Jonah** pushed that one open on his own. Clearly, the opportunity was open for **Jonah** to catch a ship to **Tarshish**, but it was not God's will for him to go.

A second lesson here is that the first step out of fellowship with God is a step down, for Jonah went **down to Joppa** and **down into** the ship fleeing the **presence of the LORD**. The notion that you can experience the abundant life Christ makes available to all children of God while in open rebellion to God's will is misguided. Rest assured, the first step out is down. And what's more, almost no one would make that step down if they could at that moment see all the consequences that would flow from their decision—in other words, if they could count the costs first. How many husbands would not stray from their wives if they could see in that moment all that they will lose? How many young people would not make decisions like they are eight feet tall and bullet proof if in the moment of decision they could see clearly the full cost that will be required of them? Jonah did not see what was to come as he stepped **down** but he was resolved to run.

Before proceeding to verse 4, a few comments about **Nineveh** are in order. God's assessment of **Nineveh** was that it was **that great city**, an indicator of its size and population. Critical scholars attack the description of **Nineveh** as **that great city**. We are told later that that **Nineveh** was "an exceeding great city of three days' journey." (see 3:3). The critic asserts that the description of the city is historically inaccurate. We may briefly make the following observations; more information is included in the introductory chapter. First, if God says it was a **great city**, rest assured, it was a **great city**. And as shown in the introductory chapter, **Nineveh** was a place of splendor and military prowess, and if not an actual capital city, was a frequent royal residence and prominent city. Further, like most major ancient cities, **Nineveh** was surrounded by smaller cities as archaeologists have confirmed, and it is likely that this was the basis for the assertion that the city was "three days' journey" (i.e., three days to walk the town). In addition, **Jonah** was not just walking the town, but was charged with getting a message to the inhabitants that must have required him to make frequent stops, gather a crowd, and deliver God's message. Finally, note that the phrase **is come up before me** may indicate angelic ministry, i.e., that angels have reported the fact of **their wickedness** to God. (e.g., Job 1:6)

> 4 But the LORD sent out a great wind into the sea, and there was a mighty tempest in the sea, so that the ship was like to be broken.

The Bible always shows God totally in control of natural forces, and this is no exception. Indeed, Nahum states, "the LORD hath his way in the whirlwind and in the storm." (Nahum 1:3) But more than that, we begin in verse 4 to see that everything and everyone in the book of Jonah—save for Jonah himself—obeyed God. Here, the wind and the sea did precisely as God desired. We read that the LORD **sent out a great wind into the sea, and there was a mighty tempest in the sea.** The result of this sudden **tempest** is **that the ship was like to be broken.** Our sin is all the worse when we cause others to endure the consequences of our poor choices. Whether knowingly or not, Jonah put everyone on board **the ship** in danger.

> 5 Then the mariners were afraid, and cried every man unto his god, and cast forth the wares that *were* in the ship into the sea, to lighten *it* of them. But Jonah was gone down into the sides of the ship; and he lay, and was fast asleep.

The experienced **mariners** or sailors were afraid, a testimony to the severity of the storm. Yet, these pagan gentiles immediately perceived the seriousness of the situation (and perhaps its divine origin), **and cried every man unto his god.** While the text does not specifically tell us where the sailors were from, the geographic location suggests some were likely Phoenician. There may have been other nationalities present since we read that each **man cried unto his god.** The Phoenicians were known as a great maritime people (see Ezekiel 26:16), and particularly relevant here, they adorned their ships with horse heads to honor Yamm, who they worshiped as the god of the sea. Surely, they must have immediately thought, Yamm who is the god of the sea can deliver us. But as we will see, the sailors soon realize their gods do not command the sea.

First they prayed, then took action **and cast forth the wares that were in the ship into the sea**, thus lightering or **to lighten** the vessel so that it did not run as deep in the water and could possibly withstand the waves. Obviously, their actions were futile since the storm was from God and they pinned their prayers on their non-existent "little g" gods. But we can at least respect the sincerity of their actions. In contrast, **Jonah**, a child of God, neither prayed nor took action. Far from recognizing this as a divine storm, **Jonah** was ignorant of what was transpiring because he **was gone down into the sides of the ship**—notice again the emphasis on his having **gone down—and he lay, and was fast asleep**. To be able to sleep through this fierce storm pictures Jonah's complete spiritual insensitivity. The sailors at least had the spiritual snap to pray, and their actions, while futile, make Jonah's inaction all the more appalling.

The Jew of Jonah's day hearing or reading this passage expected at any moment that **Jonah** would rise from his physical slumber—his spiritual stupor—and pray to the God of heaven and beg forgiveness for his sin. But as we will see, that never happened. As a believer continues stepping (down) out of fellowship with God, the believer hardens his/her heart, becoming insensitive to God's appeal for repentance and generally to the things of God, just as **Jonah** was oblivious to the storm. God's words fell on deaf ears with Jonah. The original audience of the book should have seen that their actions as a nation paralleled Jonah's. They too were asleep to God's appeal that they repent and turn back to Him.

> 6 So the shipmaster came to him, and said unto him, What meanest thou, O sleeper? arise, call upon thy God, if so be that God will think upon us, that we perish not.

The captain or **shipmaster** was desperate, for they had called on their gods for deliverance to no avail. They knew Jonah was not from their people and so the captain **came to** Jonah. With incredulity, the captain asked, **What meanest thou, O sleeper?** In other words, "How can you possibly sleep while we are all about to die?" The captain ordered Jonah to **arise** from his sleep and **call up** to his **God, if so be that God will think upon us, that we perish not**. What an incredible transformation. The pagans realized their gods cannot help them and hoped Jonah could **call** upon his **God** for help, while idolatrous Israel disregarded God and looked to the gods for help. God chased Jonah with the storm but was left standing outside the door. God then used the **shipmaster** to "get in Jonah's face" about the matter, a bleak reminder of the depth of his (and Israel's) sinful disobedience.

It was not to be lost on Jonah's original audience, or us, that the captain's words echoed Jonah's calling from God. In verse 2, God said, "Arise, go to Nineveh," as if awaking Jonah to his God-given task. And here, the captain said, **arise, call upon thy God**. But how could Jonah call upon Him whom he was fleeing? Thus, irony abounds as a pagan sailor who knew nothing of God pleaded with a prophet of Yahweh to pray for deliverance, but God's prophet would have no part with God even if it meant death. Israel as a nation, like Jonah, needed desperately to **call upon** their **God** for forgiveness and turn from their idolatry and moral decay. But they were asleep to God's pleas.

> 7 And they said every one to his fellow, Come, and let us cast lots, that we may know for whose cause this evil *is* upon us. So they cast lots, and the lot fell upon Jonah.

Their own gods failed them and **Jonah** was unwilling to pray to his God, so the pagan sailors turned to what they knew, a belief that divine will can be determined by casting **lots**. Thus, **they said every one to his fellow, Come, and let us cast lots.** Note that their purpose is **that we may know for whose cause this evil is upon us.** Again, there is irony in that the man of God continued in a spiritual stupor while the pagans rightly concluded the storm was a judgment for someone's sin. The sailors sought divine instruction. Thus **they cast lots, and the lot fell upon Jonah.** We should note that the casting of lots was in some circumstances an appropriate way to discern the will of God. We read in Joshua 18:10 how he cast lots to divide the land during the Conquest: "And Joshua cast lots for them in Shiloh before the LORD: and there Joshua divided the land unto the children of Israel according to their divisions." And in the New Testament, lots were cast to allow God to show His will in the selection of a new apostle: "And they gave forth their lots; and the lot fell upon Matthias; and he was numbered with the eleven apostles." (Acts 1:26) The Bible teaches that God determines the outcome: "The lot is cast into the lap; but the whole disposing thereof *is* of the LORD." (Proverbs 16:33)

One note of warning—we do not see the casting of lots after Acts 1 and should not place too great a weight on the historic apostolic example as a model for determining God's will thereafter, especially since in Acts 2 the Holy Spirit's ministry to the church began. I would argue that at that point, the use of lots was rendered obsolete as Christians were to follow the leading of the Spirit. In any event, **the lot fell upon Jonah** and the sailors accepted the outcome as divine, as the questions they asked of **Jonah** demonstrated. Thus far, God used a storm and the words of the gentile captain to remind Jonah of his disobedience, and now God used the lots to do the same. It would seem that Jonah had nowhere to run and hide. What a powerful conviction on Jonah to confess his sin and repent.

> 8 Then said they unto him, Tell us, we pray thee, for whose cause this evil *is* upon us; What *is* thine occupation? and whence comest thou? what *is* thy country? and of what people *art* thou? 9 And he said unto them, I *am* an Hebrew; and I fear the LORD, the God of heaven, which hath made the sea and the dry *land.* 10 Then were the men exceedingly afraid, and said unto him, Why hast thou done this? For the men knew that he fled from the presence of the LORD, because he had told them.

It was apparent to the pagan sailors that the storm was a divine response to someone's personal sin, and the lots pointed to Jonah. Thus, they interrogated Jonah to confirm his guilt, **Tell us, we pray thee, for whose cause this evil is upon us**. Desperate to quickly get to the bottom of the matter, they pressed their questions, **What is thine occupation? and whence comest thou? what is thy country? and of what people art thou?** These were not the words of careful deliberation, but questions born out of fear that the storm would imminently kill them. For the first time in the book, Jonah spoke, saying **unto them, I am an Hebrew; and I fear the LORD, the God of heaven, which hath made the sea and dry land**. We dare not miss the absurdity of Jonah's response. To this point, he did nothing that showed he **fear[ed] the LORD, the God of heaven**. That he was on the run from God dispels his statement. Jonah was right, of course, that God **made the sea and dry land**. But this knowledge should have prompted his obedience to God's call, or at least a response to the storm straight away, rather than a nap while the sailors frantically lightered the vessel to save their lives and Jonah's.

It is easy after being around church a while to pick up the spiritual lingo. We say things like "die to self," "Lord willing," "I will be praying for you," and "I am just looking for the Lord's leading." These words and phrases are good and right if they reflect our hearts. But we can put on a good show and say the right things to get the approval of people. We must remember, however, that we have an "Audience of One." Let those three words sink into the core of your being—an <u>Audience of One</u>! Our thoughts, words and actions need to please God as of a first priority, and God is not pleased with empty rhetoric no matter how eloquent. Recall Jesus' words about prayer in the Sermon on the Mount: "And when thou prayest, thou shalt not be as the hypocrites *are*: for they love to pray standing in the synagogues and in the corners of the streets, that they may be seen of men. Verily I say unto you, They have their reward." (Matthew 6:5) It is a dangerous game we play when we use vain words in a false spiritual piety. Did not God warn, "Thou shalt not take the name of the LORD thy God in vain; for the LORD will not hold him guiltless that taketh his name in vain."? (Exodus 20:7) Yet, that is exactly what disobedient Jonah did as he proclaimed his fear of the LORD in the midst of his continuing rebellion. This was nothing more than empty God-talk. It was form without reality, a parade of spiritual rhetoric devoid of substance. Yet we have a great capacity to delude ourselves by going through the spiritual motions. Jesus cut to the chase when he said that if we love him we would keep his commandments. (John 14:15) God could have said to Jonah, if you "fear" me, then stop talking and start walking. GO TO NINEVEH!

Accordingly, it is critical as we exegete the book of Jonah to see his reactions and words in context and not be misled by pious words. There are places in the book where there is a tendency among Christian readers to give Jonah too much credit based on his words. Some may argue that Jonah repented in verse 9. But we need to look beyond his words, considering what Jonah did not say as much as what he did say. And chapter 4 confirms Jonah never repented. God assessed Job (probably a contemporary of Abraham) as the most righteous living human at the time, and God's assessment was based on two facts—Job feared God and eschewed evil. Jonah, in contrast to Job, had the talk but not the walk. I am reminded of the man who declared to another his righteousness, and the other responded, "I can't hear you, your life is speaking too loud!" Jonah's words were empty, and he set himself (a member of God's chosen nation) in contrast to the sailors. But if his faith were evident before men, the sailors would not have needed to ask the barrage of questions they asked in verse 8.

Finally, note the sailors' response. **Then were the men exceedingly afraid**. The sailors saw through Jonah's words and, although the dialogue is not recorded, they must have pressed him further. Indeed, they learned that Jonah had **fled from the presence of the LORD** because **he had told them**. What we know is that Jonah told them he fled God; we do not know how much detail he provided or what "spin" he may have placed on the facts. They asked Jonah, **Why hast thou done this?** Again, there is the unmistakable irony that the pagan sailors perceived the gravity of Jonah's sin while he did not, or at least did not care. Israel had run from God for years.

> 11 Then said they unto him, What shall we do unto thee, that the sea may be calm unto us?

for the sea wrought, and was tempestuous.
12 And he said unto them, Take me up, and
cast me forth into the sea; so shall the sea be
calm unto you: for I know that for my sake
this great tempest *is* upon you. 13 Nevertheless
the men rowed hard to bring *it* to the land;
but they could not: for the sea wrought, and
was tempestuous against them. 14 Wherefore
they cried unto the LORD, and said, We
beseech thee, O LORD, we beseech thee, let
us not perish for this man's life, and lay not
upon us innocent blood: for thou, O LORD,
hast done as it pleased thee. 15 So they took
up Jonah, and cast him forth into the sea: and
the sea ceased from her raging.

The sailors sought the prophet's guidance about how to
appease the wrath of God, asking **him, What shall we do
unto thee, that the sea may be calm unto us?** Thus, by the
means of the sailors, God made another appeal to Jonah to
repent and turn from his rebellion. Although Jonah was
awakened from his slumber and admitted fleeing the
presence of God, **the sea** remained **wrought, and
...tempestuous.** The vessel and all on board remained in
imminent peril. To this point, Jonah enjoyed a captive
audience among the sailors, yet only made a passing
comment about the person and nature of the LORD.
Notwithstanding, the sailors responded to the light shown
them, both in the storm and Jonah's empty confession.
Thus again we see the irony that these sailors responded and
sought to understand what God wanted. But Jonah's
response was only resignation to his fate, telling them, **Take
me up, and cast me forth into the sea; so shall the sea be
calm unto you: for I know that for my sake this great
tempest is upon you.**

Some expositors see contrition here and compassion for the sailors as Jonah offered himself a sacrifice to appease the wrath of God, but nowhere here or anywhere in the book does Jonah confess his attitude toward God as sin. Instead, Jonah's plea for their assistance in his suicide was merely the ultimate means of fleeing God's presence to avoid addressing his sin and guilt. Jonah acknowledged the storm was on his account (the sailors already knew this because of the lots), but that is all Jonah acknowledged; Jonah did not acknowledge that he was in the wrong. Jonah was faced with a choice between death, on the one hand, and repentance and turning back to God, on the other hand. And this was the choice God put squarely before Israel as He brought them warnings through Amos, Hosea and Jonah. It is a relatively easy thing to see through Jonah and correct him, just as King David quickly judged the rich man in the prophet Nathan's story that stole the poor man's lamb. As Jonah's story unfolds before us, we are compelled to stand and exhort him: "Jonah, just confess to God you were wrong to flee His presence. Admit to God your disobedience and ask His forgiveness. Vow to God that you will go to Nineveh and deliver whatever message God has for the city." But Jonah would not hear us, as he did not hear God. He is not ready to stop running yet because in his rebellious heart he believes he is right and God is wrong.

Jonah pictured Israel, running from God and choosing death—which would eventually come at the hand of the Assyrians—over repentance and obedience toward God. But by application, is not Jonah a picture of any prodigal individual, church, or nation? We must recognize that we have it in us to be just like Jonah, indulging a rebellious heart and running from the One who loves us as His children because we do not want Him to exercise authority over us. Recall the words of rejection from Jesus' parable, "We will not have this man to reign over us." (Luke 19:14) We may not articulate our rebellion so blatantly as to say to God, "I choose death over obedience," but our actions, as Jonah's, reveal our hearts. We do well to ask, what does a prodigal Christian look like? And the answer is, "a lot like Jonah." But we run in different ways. Some prodigals run from church to church, always waxing pious when they leave (either the "Lord is leading them elsewhere" or "they are not being fed") but their rhetoric is a thin veneer for the rebellious heart beneath. Others skip out on church altogether, claiming they can worship God from their bass boat on the lake on Sunday morning, construing church as man's idea and not Jesus' personal construction project for which he died.

A stack of books would not suffice to catalogue the myriad paths traversed by prodigals, defying God to their own hurt. God draws a picture for us. "Look at Jonah," He says. And may I say, churches and even nations can be prodigals. Nineveh was the prodigal city, but its repentance and turning away from sin is a testament to us that the very worst prodigal can respond to God in contrition and obedience rather than fleeing. In our precarious time, as foundations crumble (see Psalm 11:3), we must seriously wrestle with the question of prodigal churches. Many churches embrace the world and reject God. Of course, its members do not say it that way, for prodigals never own it until they turn back to God. Yet their preachers carry the Bible to the pulpit as a prop for their performance, squandering their opportunity to open it and tell the people what God said. They, like Jonah, had a call to "arise" and "go" but refused. There are many ways a church can go prodigal, but chiefly when they abandon God's Word and the central command to love God and others in all things.

We must also wrestle with the question of whether the United States is a prodigal, just as Israel was called out by the history of Jonah to see itself as prodigal. God did not abandon the United States, but the United States told God to stay out of its public schools and universities because God has no place in education. The United States told God to keep out of its courts, which should not display the Ten Commandments. The United States told God to stay out of its marriages because He has no place defining marriage or telling people to honor their commitments. The United States told God to stay out of procreation because when children in the womb are inconvenient they should be freely discarded. The United States told God to keep out of science because evolution was our belief of choice despite the overwhelming evidence against it. Prodigals of any sort face a choice, judgment or turning back to God. As Paul wrote, "For the wrath of God is revealed from heaven against all ungodliness and unrighteousness of men, who hold the truth in unrighteousness." (Romans 1:18)

While we might expect the pagan sailors, fully aware of Jonah's guilt and the resultant tempest that threatened their lives, to eagerly throw Jonah overboard, they did not. In fact, **the men rowed hard to bring** the ship **to the land**. Again, we find great irony, both because Jonah showed no compassion for them, and as the book unfolds, we will see that Jonah had no compassion for the Ninevites either. In chapter 4, Jonah relished the opportunity to sit in a place of comfort and watch the destruction of Nineveh. Jonah believed they "had it coming to them." Yet, these sailors showed compassion for Jonah, who undoubtedly deserved God's temporal wrath for his disobedience. **But** try as they might **they could not** get the ship to shore because **the sea wrought, and was tempestuous against them**. The sea, like every "character" in the book except Jonah, obeyed God, who would force Jonah to make his choice between death and repentance and not allow the sailors, however well intentioned, to help Jonah escape his predicament.

Once the sailors realized they could not get to shore, **they cried** or prayed **unto the LORD, and said, We beseech thee, O LORD, we beseech thee, let us not perish for this man's life, and lay not upon us innocent blood: for thou, O LORD, hast done as it pleased thee.** Jonah never honored their request to pray (v. 6) to the LORD, but in another layer of irony, the sailors then prayed—no doubt for the first time in their lives—**unto the LORD.** They came to faith in the one true God despite Jonah, not because of Jonah. They recognized God's complete sovereignty over the entire situation (**thou...hast done as it pleased thee**). They feared that if they acceded to Jonah's plea and tossed him overboard, God would **lay...upon** them the **innocent blood** of Jonah. Of course, Jonah is not **innocent** before God, but he had done them no evil directly, and likely Jonah told them about fleeing God but not *why* he fled, namely his refusal to go to Nineveh. That the sailors recognized God's sovereignty and hand of judgment enough to ask God not to hold them accountable for what they feel they must do is striking. Having prayed desperately to God for deliverance, **they took up Jonah, and cast him forth into the sea: and the sea ceased from her raging.** The cessation of the tempest confirms that God would not hold the sailors guilty for the life of Jonah.

> 16 Then the men feared the LORD exceedingly, and offered a sacrifice unto the LORD, and made vows. 17 Now the LORD had prepared a great fish to swallow up Jonah. And Jonah was in the belly of the fish three days and three nights.

The sailors responded appropriately to God's mercy in the context of their limited knowledge of God, and in stark contrast to Jonah's response to God. Jonah voiced the words, "I fear the LORD" (v. 9), but God affirmed that **the men feared the LORD** exceedingly. More than that, the sailors responded in worship and **offered a sacrifice unto the LORD, and made vows**. A vow is not a promise to repay God with money, but to publicly praise Him for His deliverance. Psalm 66 provides an example; there, David spoke of paying his "vows" by providing a public testimony to what God did for him:

> <u>Psalm 66:13</u> I will go into thy house with burnt offerings: I will pay thee my vows, <u>14</u> Which my lips have uttered, and my mouth hath spoken, when I was in trouble. <u>15</u> I will offer unto thee burnt sacrifices of fatlings, with the incense of rams; I will offer bullocks with goats. Selah. <u>16</u> Come *and* hear, all ye that fear God, and I will declare what he hath done for my soul.

God's prophet would not speak to Nineveh of God but the sailors would take God's mighty deliverance with them to every port and speak of how He delivered them. If Jonah's embarrassing response to God's instructions were not enough, certainly the positive response of the sailors should have convicted Israel of their idolatry and moral decay.

When hope is lost and no help is deserved, we find God longsuffering and merciful, even in the face of obstinate disobedience. Contrary to everything Jonah deserved, God brought deliverance. We read that **now the LORD had prepared a great fish to swallow Jonah.** Jonah did not repent, nor yet even pray, but God graciously gave him more time.

This was underserved mercy, but does not mean that Jonah was completely unscathed. Had he repented topside, he could have returned to land in the comfort of the vessel. Instead, he **was in the belly of the fish three days and three nights**. More details about Jonah's strange journey by fish will follow in the next chapter, but this summary statement reminds us that no matter how far we have fallen, God can reach us in His mercy. Truly, God chased Jonah with mercy and grace. If only Jonah would have turned back to God, he could have proclaimed with King David, "surely goodness and mercy shall follow me all the days of my life." (Psalm 23:6)

One final note. I will not try to explain here how God could use a fish by natural means to deliver Jonah. I am satisfied that it was a miracle. Some commentators have demonstrated by historical examples that men have been swallowed at sea by large sharks and whales and survived. There is ample evidence, for example, that a sperm whale could have swallowed Jonah, by nature of its size and its presence in the Mediterranean Sea. We do not need to argue that Jonah was just one of several men to have been swallowed by a fish and survive, and certainly there is no account of a man spending three days in a whale and surviving. I take it simply as a miracle of God, which I believe is exactly how we are intended to take it. This was God's supernatural deliverance that only He could provide, just as the storm and other elements in the history of Jonah were plainly supernatural and intended to be accepted as such.

Closing

We have all heard the expression, "he is trying to dig his way out of a hole." The problem is the person doing the digging is oblivious. If he realizes there is a problem, his solution will be to add a second shovel. The only way to turn around from the insanity is to first take stock and realize where you are. In the parable of the prodigal son, after the prodigal exhausted his inheritance and was demoted from his station in life to tending swine, we read, "when he came to himself, he said, How many hired servants of my father's have bread enough to spare, and I perish with hunger!" (Luke 15:17) In that moment, "when he came to himself" and not a moment before, he realized his condition. No one ever turns back to the Father without first realizing their condition. Jonah did not see it; he was still digging. But what about you? You cannot know if you are chasing Jonah unless you take stock of your condition. While we might not always like what we will hear, we do well to be open to what our friends and family think. "Faithful are the wounds of a friend..." (Proverbs 27:6) If we are trying to dig out of a hole, those closest to us know it. Stop digging and look up.

Application Points

- **MAIN PRINCIPLE:** Genuine spirituality is not established by our confessional theology (e.g., I fear the Lord) but our experiential, proof in the pudding theology (e.g., thoughts, words and actions), and especially our obedience to God's will as it is explicitly revealed in the Bible.

- Believers who have sinned against God either run to Him for forgiveness or run from Him.

- God chases sinners, calling upon them to repent.

- Just because an opportunity is available does not, in and of itself, mean it is God's will for you.

Discussion Questions

1. Why do you think the message God had for the Ninevites is not set forth in chapter 1?

2. Why did Jonah run from God's presence?

3. Have you run from God's presence, and if so, how did you run and why did you run?

4. Why did God chase Jonah and by what means might God chase us?

5. Why are we so effective at seeing the faults in others and not our own?

6. Jonah found ready passage to Spain. How can we know when an opportunity open to us is from God or not?

7. What are ways in which we can emulate what we think Christians are supposed to do or say without those actions and words really reflecting our hearts?

8. Thinking about how your thoughts, words and actions play out before a Holy God, what is the significance of the phrase "Audience of One" to you?

9. Do you see something of yourself in Jonah?

Chapter 3

Jonah's Unrepentant Heart

Know anyone that only calls you when they need something? Years pass in silence but when they get their tail in a crack, the phone rings. "How are you doing?...It's been so long, I wish we could get together sometime...Hey, I heard you went to law school and I'm having this issue with my ex...." And you are like, "who is this again?" Perhaps it is a family member you have not seen since 1982. "Jeanie, hey, its Billy... You know, your cousin Billy... Yeah... Yeah... You're a nurse, right?... I have this infection on my...." The sad reality is that too many Christians are strangers to God until they have a problem. So how does that conversation go? "Most awesome heavenly Father God, thou art... awesome... heavenly... thy will be done... this is Billy... I need a" and we can fill in the blank. No amount of King James English will repair Billy's prayer because all Billy cares about is what God can give him, just like that person we get a call from out of the blue who has no sincere interest in us except for what they need at that moment. Of course, the Bible says to "come boldly unto the throne of grace, that we may obtain mercy, and find grace to help in time of need." (Hebrews 4:16) But the Bible presumes regular communications. If we only talk to God when we think we need something, then all we will ever see is our need and not our God. And as we will find in chapter 2, Jonah prayed, not because he desired God, but only because he desired God's deliverance.

Outline

JONAH'S UNREPENTANT HEART (ch. 2)
  a. Jonah prays because of his affliction (2:1-4)
  b. Jonah hits bottom but no repentance (2:5-7)
  c. Jonah talks the talk (2:8)
  d. Jonah makes a vow (2:9)
  e. God intervenes for Jonah (2:10)

Scripture and Comments

As a preliminary matter, chapter 2 contains a psalm, and as such, it is Hebrew poetry. I have formatted the lines accordingly. Moreover, Jonah's psalm follows a familiar format of other Hebrew psalms where the worshiper summarizes God's deliverance before explaining the peril they faced and making a plea for deliverance, followed by a giving of thanks or vow to glorify God for their deliverance. We see examples in Psalms 18 and 116, and indeed, many of the psalms contain some of these elements, e.g., Psalm 66 (vow) and 116 (summary then peril). Jonah knew the Psalms and he knew how to emulate the heartfelt praise in those psalms. Despite this, a careful look at the text bears out that as much as we want to see Jonah repent, his prayer was merely one for deliverance. While superficially the words were laudable (recall his confession in 1:9), notably lacking was any admission of guilt, any confession of sin, any request for forgiveness, or a promise to go to Nineveh.

63

> Jonah 2:1 Then Jonah prayed unto the LORD
> his God out of the fish's belly, 2 And said,
>
> I cried by reason of mine affliction unto the
> LORD,
>
> and he heard me;
>
> out of the belly of hell cried I,
>
> and thou heardest my voice.

This chapter begins with an editorial comment, **then Jonah prayed unto the LORD his God out of the fish's belly. Jonah... cried by reason of** his **affliction** or peril **unto the LORD.** At the brink of death by drowning, Jonah was swallowed by a great fish, and from within the fish, he prayed for deliverance. **Jonah** should have confessed his sin and cried out for forgiveness while he was on the ship but he refused. Now that he was in imminent peril, he pleaded for physical deliverance. This is the all too familiar plea of desperation without contrition that is reminiscent of the time of the Judges. (e.g., Judges 3:8-9, 14-15; 4:2-3; 6:6-8) Yet, God in His goodness, **heard** the prayer, meaning that God responded favorably to Jonah's plea. In this, God extends underserved mercy to the prodigal.

Notice the parallelism with the first and third lines of poetry, and the second and fourth lines. This is a common feature of Hebrew poetry—not rhyme of word but "rhyme" of idea—and it can aid our understanding. We also need to be mindful that as poetry, figurative language is employed to convey the gravity and emotion of the experience. This means that we should be wary of taking every expression in a rigidly literal way, missing the poetic use of metaphors and other figures of speech. And the key to distinguishing the literal from the figurative always lies in a careful examination of the context.

Jonah explained that he **cried by reason of mine affliction** in the first line, then **out of the belly of hell cried I** in the third line. The term **hell** is the Hebrew term *sheol*, which refers to the place of the dead or the underworld. Strong's defines the term as "Hades or the world of the dead (as if a subterranean retreat), including its accessories and inmates:-grave, hell, pit." It is helpful to see its similar usage in other passages:

> Psalm 18:5 The sorrows of **hell** compassed me about: the snares of death prevented me.

> Psalm 86:13 For great *is* thy mercy toward me: and thou hast delivered my soul from the lowest **hell**.

> Isaiah 38:18 For the **grave** cannot praise thee, death can *not* celebrate thee: they that go down into the pit cannot hope for thy truth.

> Job 7:9 *As* the cloud is consumed and vanisheth away: so he that goeth down to the **grave** shall come up no *more*.

Returning then to Jonah's plea, he prayed from **the belly of hell**. He was not literally in the place of the dead (since he was alive and praying), but in the **belly** of the fish. Because he contemplated his imminent death in that moment, he likened the fish's **belly** to being in the center of the underworld or the place of the dead. His poetic language was all the more fitting in this context because the ancients believed that *sheol* was below the ocean floor. In any event, **Jonah** was not in *sheol* but the fish's **belly**, which he believed would prove to be his grave. He saw death at the door, as it were, and so he prayed. This is somewhat inconsistent since it was **Jonah** who asked in chapter 1 to be thrown overboard.

There, he was ostensibly ready to die. He recalled that God **heard me** and **heardest my voice**. God delivered Jonah in response to his prayer. We can say one positive thing about **Jonah**. As bad off as he was, when completely cornered by his circumstances he had the sense to finally pray. But as Christians we ought to be praying before we are in the fish.

> 3 For thou hadst cast me into the deep,
>
> in the midst of the seas:
>
> and the floods compassed me about:
>
> all thy billows and thy waves passed over me.

As we witnessed in Jonah 1, Jonah volunteered to be thrown in the water. Yet here, Jonah would make God responsible, asserting that God **hadst cast me into the deep** waters. Remember that the reason Jonah asked to be thrown into the sea was because he did not want to repent. He, as representative of Israel, chose death to repentance. Jonah resigned to his fate and told the sailors what to do. It is no doubt true that God worked through the sailors, but there is more than a hint of "this is not my fault, it's God's doing" in Jonah's words, the very opposite of a repentant heart. Jonah found himself in **the deep** water **in the midst of the seas** (specifically, the Mediterranean). Perhaps he struggled to swim but the water was too strong as **the floods compassed** him **about**. Jonah sank as the **billows and...waves passed over** his head, perhaps looking up to the surface as he descended the ocean depths. Note that Jonah said the overwhelming water was **thy billows and thy waves**. He recognized God's role in the event, but did not recognize his own culpability. Jonah was drowning and would be dead in a matter of moments. Even here, in the very teeth of death, Jonah would not repent.

> 4 Then I said, I am cast out of thy sight;
> yet I will look again toward thy holy temple.

Notwithstanding his lack of confession and repentance, Jonah expressed confidence that he would be delivered. Jonah knew his God is a God of mercy, which of course, is at the heart of why he refused to obey God and preach to Nineveh (he feared they might repent and receive God's mercy). Thus, he recognized that he was **cast out of** God's **sight**. Of course, Jonah must have known that the creator God (see 1:9) could see him anywhere, for there is no place hidden from God. What Jonah did poetically was to liken his grave in the depths of the ocean to being banished from God's presence above the water's surface. But again, we must remember that it was Jonah who chose to flee God's presence when he was commanded to go to Nineveh. It was Jonah who chose to flee again by telling the sailors to throw him overboard. God did not **cast out** Jonah. So here, there is still the hint of Jonah seeing himself as the victim. We have an amazing capacity to do the most immoral things and somehow seek to ameliorate the effects by labeling ourselves a victim. The Hollywood types, when called to the mat over their outrageous behavior, enroll in rehabilitation centers for treatment. What they did was not their fault; rather, they are the unfortunate victim of an addiction or the like. Jonah called on God but still refused to take responsibility for his disobedience.

Yet in his watery exile, Jonah was confident that he **will look again toward** God's **holy temple**, in other words, that he would get a reprieve. Jonah's example and God's deliverance of Jonah was a clarion call to Israel to turn back to God and call upon Him. If God rescued Jonah, he would surely rescue Israel. May I say that we too can find ourselves drowning in our circumstances. We can have chased after Jonah's example and stepped away from the will of God to the point we might as well be in a fish's belly.   But like

Jonah, we must remember that God is longsuffering and merciful. We must see in the mirror the reality of who and where we are, like the prodigal son who came to himself, and recognize when it is time to fall down at the feet of God for mercy and restoration. But more than a plea for mercy, we must confess our wrong against God and seek forgiveness. (1 John 1:9)

> 5 The waters compassed me about, even to
>   the soul:
>
> the depth closed me round about,
>
> the weeds were wrapped about my head.

Jonah's disobedience brought him near the ocean's bottom. Sin always takes us farther than we want to go, and so it was with Jonah. **The waters** completely **compassed** or engulfed Jonah, **even to the soul**, meaning that he was in imminent danger of losing his life. He wrote that the **depth** of the sea **closed...round about** him and that he descended to the point that the **weeds** or seaweeds on the ocean floor began to be **wrapped** or entangled **about his head**. Thus, as Jonah neared the ocean floor, the ocean floor as an extension of *sheol* "grabbed" him to draw him into the grave. There was no escape. By any natural assessment of the situation, it was hopeless. Jonah was doomed to drown and never be seen again. Yet these are the circumstances when the hand of God may lift us up.

> 6 I went down to the bottoms of the
>   mountains;
>
> the earth with her bars was about me for ever:
>
> yet hast thou brought up my life from
>   corruption, O LORD my God.

The **mountains** are pictured as being rooted to the ocean floor; Jonah went all the way **down to the bottoms** or roots **of the mountains**, meaning he reached the deepest point possible. Sheol, beneath the ocean floor, was viewed as being gated on the ocean floor **with her bars** that wrap **about** and bind Jonah captive **for ever**. The grave would not permit an escape, and thus Jonah, in the very grip of death, felt those **bars** binding him (see Job 38:10; Psalm 9:13; Isaiah 38:10). Yet at that very moment God delivered him. Jonah wrote first of the deliverance, then in the next verse that this deliverance was an answer to his desperate prayer. The LORD...**God**, Jonah tells us, **brought up** his **life from corruption**. The term **corruption** is often translated as "pit" and used in connection with *sheol.* Having been so rescued from certain death, it is as if Jonah had been resurrected from the pit.

A natural question here is did Jonah die? The language, **brought up my life from corruption**, could be taken to mean Jonah died and was resurrected. The language can also be understood figuratively or poetically, which is natural in the context of a psalm like Jonah's. The idea would simply be that when Jonah was "as good as dead" and "all hope was lost," God rescued him. This is my view, but many solid conservative commentators take it that Jonah died and was resurrected (e.g., J. Vernon McGee, Henry Morris). In their view, since Jesus established that Jonah's time in the fish and his deliverance pictured His own death, burial, and resurrection, it is fitting that Jonah actually died. Read Jesus' words in this regard:

> Matthew 12:39 But he answered and said unto them, An evil and adulterous generation seeketh after a sign; and there shall no sign be

given to it, but the sign of the prophet Jonas: 40 For as Jonas was three days and three nights in the whale's belly; so shall the Son of man be three days and three nights in the heart of the earth. 41 The men of Nineveh shall rise in judgment with this generation, and shall condemn it: because they repented at the preaching of Jonas; and, behold, a greater than Jonas *is* here.

As discussed in the introductory chapter, this passage reflects Jesus' understanding of Jonah, and accordingly informs our interpretation. We will see in the next chapter that Jonah provided minimal revelation from God to the people of Nineveh—a bare warning of impending judgment—yet they renounced their sins and repented. In contrast, the Israel of Jonah's day had substantial revelation from God through Amos, Hosea and Jonah, but ultimately did not repent and fell in judgment to the Assyrians. Likewise, the generation of Israel during Jesus' earthly ministry received "Son" revelation (see Hebrews 1:1-2) and rejected God's message. Thus, Jesus applies the message of Jonah to the generation that witnessed his earthly ministry. Just as the Ninevites' repentance served as a condemnation of Israel's refusal to repent in the time of Jonah, so also did their repentance serve as a condemnation of the generation alive during Jesus' ministry for their failure to repent since a prophet greater than Jonah (i.e., more and better revelation of God) was among them. Jesus' resurrection, of which Jonah's time in the fish and deliverance to land is a type, would vindicate all that he taught, and especially his Messianic claims that Israel characteristically rejected.

Turning then to the question of whether Jonah drowned, the difficulty is that the text of Jonah 2 does not clearly say.

That Jonah prayed from the belly of the fish tends to suggest he did not drown but was preserved alive in the fish. And the language, **brought up my life from corruption**, can have the figurative sense of saving Jonah at the very last moment. Nor is it necessary that Jonah actually died for Jesus to use Jonah's time in the fish and deliverance to land as a type for his death, burial and resurrection since types do not require exact correlation of details. In typology, a prior event foreshadows a future event, but does not necessarily duplicate it. To argue that Jonah must have died to accurately picture Christ's death would suggest that Abraham must have actually sacrificed Isaac to foreshadow Christ's sacrifice, which we know is not the case.

Moreover, the fish is a picture of the tomb, and if Jonah died in the fish, then we have a burial, death, resurrection (in that order), which does not really help Jonah's experience to better correlate with Jesus' experience. We must remember that the psalm is poetry and it uses poetic devices such as the figurative language of the grave and the roots of the **mountains** and the **bars** of *sheol*; we need not read Jonah's references to the grave in such a wooden literal sense. What he conveyed is that the watery depths and the fish's belly were like a grave and but for God's deliverance would have been his grave. But with all this said, whether or not you believe Jonah died in the fish does not affect the interpretation of the rest of the book or the passage in Matthew 12.

> 7 When my soul fainted within me
> I remembered the LORD:
> and my prayer came in unto thee,
> into thine holy temple.

Jonah prayed at the very brink of death, **when** his **soul** or life **fainted within** him, and his prayer was heard. As he was fading, he **remembered the LORD**, meaning that he thought to pray, and his **prayer came in unto** God in His **holy temple**. In other words, Jonah's words were favorably received by God. It is possible that Jonah had in mind the **holy temple** in Jerusalem, where God's presence manifested, but more likely Jonah had in mind God's heavenly abode.

> <u>8</u> They that observe lying vanities
> forsake their own mercy.

Jonah basically said that God was the only source of mercy and salvation. **They that observe** or worship **lying** vanities, a reference to powerless idols, **forsake** or forfeit the **mercy** that could be theirs from God. This statement is theologically accurate, and taken alone, it makes Jonah sound quite spiritual. But this is mere self-righteousness, much like Jonah's answer to the sailor's questions in chapter 1. This verse tells us that Jonah's attitude since the first verse in the book has not changed. Jonah did not see Israel as idolatrous, but did see Gentiles like the sailors and the Ninevites as idolaters who **observe lying vanities** and thus are not worthy of **mercy**. Yet so far, it has been the sailors and not Jonah that acted admirably.

Moreover, what Jonah reaffirmed here, in the midst of his undeserved deliverance, is that the Ninevites should not be delivered, and by implication there is no basis for God requiring Jonah to go preach to them. God just needed to destroy them and be done with it. As the expression goes, "Jonah cannot hear himself." His words betray his spiritual delusion. The empty rhetoric is no disguise for his rebellious heart, which is still at odds with God's will for Nineveh. Jonah could not see the reality of who he was, but contemptuously looked down his nose at the Gentiles. Likewise, the nation of Israel could pick out the sins of the Gentiles but was blind to its own, which indisputably involved rank sin and unbridled idolatry. (see Hosea 4:17, 8:4) Recall Jesus' words: "O ye hypocrites, ye can discern the face of the sky; but can ye not discern the signs of the times?" (Matthew 16:3)

> 9 But I will sacrifice unto thee
> with the voice of thanksgiving;
> I will pay that that I have vowed.
> Salvation is of the LORD.

In contrast to the people of Nineveh who worshiped idols, Jonah vowed that if he was delivered he would **sacrifice unto God with the voice of thanksgiving**. Remember that a common component of worship for the Jews was the notion of making a vow when praying for a need or deliverance. The vow was that once delivered the worshiper would go to the Temple and in the presence of the congregation make a thank offering (this type of offering would be eaten as a communal meal among the worshipers) and publicly proclaim what God had done in his life. In modern times, we might call this giving a testimony, although too often we associate a testimony only with the gift of salvation from sin's penalty and not God's Hand in our daily lives.

Thus, Jonah vowed to God to offer a public testimony, promising that he **will pay that that I have vowed**. He said then and would later proclaim publicly at the Temple, **salvation is of the LORD**. By **salvation** he meant physical rescue or deliverance from peril. Again, the words sound good and right, but where is the recognition that Jonah brought about his own circumstances? Where is the promise to make a burnt offering for his sin? He does not mention a sin offering because he has not acknowledged his sin. Jonah will gladly pay his vow, but what will he tell the congregation about how and why this peril from which God delivered him happened in the first place? Moreover, and perhaps most importantly, observe that Jonah's vow did not include going to Nineveh to take them God's message. This would have been a fitting time to say "yes sir" to God's command to arise and go.

In any event, we do well to learn from Jonah's negative example. God will allow us to sin. He gives us volition in that regard, but also allows us to face the consequences of our actions. How easy it is in the midst of the consequences to pray for a lifting of the consequences without addressing the root problem—sin. Christians who are growing learn to see and address the root issues of life. Christians who continue as spiritual babes see only their circumstances and tend to walk in a cycle of consequences. Babies make messes.

> 10 And the LORD spake unto the fish, and it vomited out Jonah upon the dry land.

God gave Jonah the undeserved mercy Jonah would deny the people of Nineveh. Again we see that every "character" in the story was obedient to God's will except Jonah. God **spake unto the fish** the command to deliver Jonah to the shore, **and** the fish **vomited Jonah upon the dry land**. Jonah's prayer for deliverance was answered with a second chance at life. The hero of Jonah 2 is not the prophet but the prophet's God, rich in mercy. Jeremiah's words are surely appropriate commentary here:

> Lamentations 3:21 This I recall to my mind, therefore have I hope. 22 *It is of* the LORD'S

> mercies that we are not consumed, because
> his compassions fail not. 23 *They are* new
> every morning: great *is* thy faithfulness.

There is a powerful lesson here for us about the character of God as presented in the Bible. There are many who see the God of the Old Testament as different in character than the God of the New Testament (arguing as if there were two "gods"). Some even disregard the Old Testament, or feel the need to try to defend God's actions there. However, one of God's perfections (some use the term "attributes") is that He is immutable, that is, who He is never changes. James exalts the "Father of lights, with whom is no variableness, neither shadow of turning." (James 1:17) Those who think that the Old Testament presents a different God are misguided. It is true that many Old Testament passages present the justice and wrath of God, but to say that God as presented in the New Testament exhibits a different character (i.e., primarily love) is to ignore much of the Old and New Testament. The various perfections of God are presented throughout the Bible and we cannot view God in light of only a single perfection or a single passage of Scripture. To do so is to render the person of God a one-dimensional caricature of who He is, a non-person. In Jonah we see God's discipline and sovereignty, but also His grace, mercy and love, both for Jonah and the Gentiles in the story.

Closing

There is an expression commonly used in the practice of law—"form over substance." It often has to do with meeting the technical requirements of the law while evading the spirit of the law. There are a great many "form over substance" Christians and they may not even be aware of it.

Their lives honor the outward "stuff" of what the Christian walk should entail, like taking on certain activities, church attendance, singing, praying, giving, etc. But God is interested in a changed life. Jonah mastered the externalities but as soon as God's will clashed with Jonah's will, Jonah's spirituality fell apart and he ran when he should have embraced the opportunity for God to change him because that is how growth happens. The problem with form over substance is anyone can do it—even those that reject Christ. But what a rare gem genuine life change is. Not just a detail and wax job, or moving around the furniture in the room, but a brick-by-brick reconstruction from the inside out where we allow God by His Spirit to chisel away at the old and build the new. "For we are his workmanship..." (Ephesians 2:10) Recall Paul's words to the Romans, "And be not conformed to this world: but be ye transformed by the renewing of your mind, that ye may prove what *is* that good, and acceptable, and perfect, will of God." (Romans 12:2) And again, "be renewed in the spirit of your mind." (Ephesians 4:23) When we let God do the building, we take on the substance and not merely the form of what Christianity is all about. Then, when the call to Nineveh is given, we go.

Application Points

- **MAIN PRINCIPLE:** We should pursue God with the whole of our lives and not only seek His face when we have a need.

- We should not be form over substance Christians, emulating the walk and talk but not be transformed from the inside out to be more and more like Jesus Christ.

Discussion Questions

1. Does Jonah's prayer reflect repentance and a turning back to God?

2. In view of Jonah's conduct in chapter 1, what should be included in his prayer in chapter 2?

3. Why did God permit Jonah to be thrown overboard?

4. Would we be better off as Christians if God stopped us from our mistakes?

5. What do you think of when you hear the phrase "form over substance" Christian?

6. Do you think Jonah died and was resurrected? Why or why not?

7. What positive things can we learn from Jonah about a prayer for deliverance or prayer for a great need in our life?

8. Is it appropriate for Christians to make a vow as Jonah does in chapter 2, or as David does in Psalm 66?

9. What would it look like for a Christian to pay a vow made in prayer?

Chapter 4

Jonah's Unfaithful Heart

A lifestyle practice of diligently engaging the Word of God is a road less traveled by. Diligently engaging the Word of God is much more and much bigger than mere study. One may pursue a study of literature or history or mathematics in an academic setting, but to embark upon this road is to step into the classroom of life with a new paradigm for living. It is setting out on a faith-driven quest for a deeper knowledge of God. The path is often a steep climb and the trip is not a short one. It is a marathon rather than a short sprint. The Bible is learned as the words on the pages sink deep within and become the fabric of our being in the process of applying God's thinking to the reality around us and in all the decisions and responses of daily living.

May I say that it is easy to embrace what we already agree with—to embrace that which affirms us. But what do we do when God's Word requires us to do a 180 or leave our comfort zone? That's when our profession gets tested. What about when God tells us to go to Nineveh and we do not want to? So in truth, the question we face really is, "Do I want to change?" In this third chapter, Jonah came to decision time once again with a renewed opportunity to obey God's Word not only in his actions, but in his heart.

Outline

JONAH'S UNFAITHFUL HEART (ch. 3)

a. Jonah heralds the destruction of Nineveh (3:1-4)

b. Every man, woman and beast repents and mourns the evil and violence of Nineveh (3:5-9)

c. God intervenes for Nineveh (3:10)

Scripture and Comments

After Jonah's shocking failure to follow the Lord's command to go to Nineveh and deliver the Lord's message to those people, followed by the Lord's dramatic rescue of Jonah from a lonely death at sea, the circumstance of Jonah's original disobedience was recreated. It seems this is a tool God uses in the instruction of His children. In the New Testament, while Jesus endured a farce of a trial at the hands of his accusers, Peter denied him three times. We read in John 18:18: "And the servants and officers stood there, who had made a fire of coals; for it was cold: and they warmed themselves: and Peter stood with them, and warmed himself." The word "coals" is the Greek *anthrakia*, used only here and in John 21:9 in the New Testament. We read in John 18:25 that while Simon Peter warmed himself by the coals he denied being Jesus' disciple. After the resurrection, and in what serves as an epilogue to John's Gospel, Jesus recreated the scene, calling his disciples from their fishing to join him on the shore: "As soon then as they were come to land, they saw a fire of coals there, and fish laid thereon, and bread." (John 21:9) Around the warm fire of coals, Jesus fed them and challenged Peter three times with the question, "lovest thou me?" And by way of this circling back to the circumstance of Peter's denial, Peter was restored. Jonah 3 presents Jonah's chance for restoration as God recreates the circumstance of his failure, and by application is a clarion call to Israel, people, churches and nations who have slid into rebellion to return to a gracious and merciful God.

> Jonah 3:1 And the word of the LORD came unto Jonah the second time, saying, 2 Arise, go unto Nineveh, that great city, and preach unto it the preaching that I bid thee. 3 So Jonah arose, and went unto Nineveh, according to the word of the LORD. Now Nineveh was an exceeding great city of three days' journey.

God's command in Jonah 1:2 was, "Arise, go to Nineveh, that great city, and cry against it..." Now, **the word of the LORD came unto Jonah the second time**. Jonah's prophetic calling was repeated, **Arise, go unto Nineveh, that great city, and preach unto it the preaching that I bid thee**. To his credit, this time Jonah obeyed. Based on what happened previously, Jonah knew he could not evade his calling. The consequence or fruit of Jonah's obedience was God's business, not Jonah's. For Jonah's task was only to faithfully deliver **the preaching that I bid thee**. God's instructions to those who would stand and speak for God never changed. It is always the job of the prophet, and by modern day application the preacher or teacher, to faithfully deliver God's Word. In the calling of the prophet Ezekiel (see Ezekiel 1-3), for instance, God told Ezekiel in chapter 3:

<u>Ezekiel 3:17</u> Son of man, I have made thee a watchman unto the house of Israel: therefore hear the word at my mouth, and give them warning from me. <u>18</u> When I say unto the wicked, Thou shalt surely die; and thou givest him not warning, nor speakest to warn the wicked from his wicked way, to save his life; the same wicked *man* shall die in his iniquity; but his blood will I require at thine hand. <u>19</u> Yet if thou warn the wicked, and he turn not from his wickedness, nor from his wicked way, he shall die in his iniquity; but thou hast delivered thy soul.

And in the next 2 verses in Ezekiel, God repeated the warning to Ezekiel in order to be absolutely clear that his responsibility was to faithfully deliver God's message. Like Jonah and like Ezekiel, we too have a message we are all called to faithfully deliver. The good news we have is that a person can become a child of God by placing their faith in Jesus Christ as their personal sin bearer on the basis of Jesus' death, burial, and resurrection. Our desire after we have completed the race before us should be to hear the words, "well done, good and <u>faithful</u> servant."

Jonah was obedient here, in a way. We read, **So Jonah arose, and went unto Nineveh, according to the word of the LORD.** But Jonah never repented, and that will become clear in Chapter 4 where Jonah told God he wanted the people of Nineveh to perish. Jonah's obedience here is purely external. He is not of one accord with God's purposes. Most ministers of God's Word pray that those who hear will be responsive, but it will become evident Jonah despised his task and his audience, thus his preaching in Nineveh issued from an unfaithful heart. God is not on Jonah's side, and he resented it. The problem, of course, is that Jonah was not on God's side. God's appeal to Jonah was not only to obey outwardly, but to be likeminded with His purposes. Only then could Jonah be restored.

People can fake godliness, deceiving others and themselves through purely external actions. We have an idea in our minds of what the Christian walk looks like and we can emulate it. But neither we nor Jonah can hide from God our true heart motivations. Much of Jesus' famous Sermon on the Mount (Matthew 5-7) contrasted the external righteousness of the scribes and Pharisees with true righteousness. That is why Jesus made the counter-cultural statement: "For I say unto you, That except your righteousness shall exceed the righteousness of the scribes and Pharisees, ye shall in no case enter into the kingdom of heaven." (Matthew 5:20) Jesus then illustrated his point with several examples in the general form, "Ye have heard that it was said by them of old time...but I say unto you...." (Matthew 5:21-22) In each case, Jesus contrasted purely external obedience to internal obedience from the heart, e.g., "thou shalt not kill" contrasted with "whosoever is angry with his brother without a cause shall be in danger of the judgment." Merely going through the motions is not faithful obedience, and Jonah was going through the motions. Neither our walk nor our worship should be purely external, but should flow from an obedient heart.

We next read, **Now Nineveh was an exceeding great** or large **city of three days' journey.** Critical scholars have expended great effort criticizing the description of the city as a **great city of three days' journey.** A perfectly reasonable explanation, demonstrated by the archaeology and the reference in Genesis 10 to cities surrounding Nineveh, is that Jonah preached through Nineveh and several smaller towns in close proximity (i.e., Metropolitan Nineveh). It may also be that the description contemplates the time it would take Jonah to walk throughout the city delivering his message, basically street by street.

> 4 And Jonah began to enter into the city a day's journey, and he cried, and said, Yet forty days, and Nineveh shall be overthrown. 5 So the people of Nineveh believed God, and proclaimed a fast, and put on sackcloth, from the greatest of them even to the least of them.

God's message through Jonah was a simple one. We read that as **Jonah began to enter into the city** of Nineveh **a day's journey**, he delivered God's succinct message, **Yet forty days, and Nineveh shall be overthrown**. The message constituted only five words in the Hebrew. There were no gimmicks, just the Word of God proclaimed, and the positive response was immediate and profound. In fact, Jonah's message was positively received from the first day of his preaching, during **a day's journey**. We are informed that the **people of Nineveh believed God, and proclaimed a fast, and put on sackcloth, from the greatest of them even to the least of them**. There was both inward reception and outward reflection in their proclaiming **a fast** and wearing **sackcloth**, signs of genuine remorse over their sin and repentance. And it was not an isolated pocket of revival, but instead the response was universal, **from the greatest of them even to the least of them**.

But what did they believe? Certainly they believed that the God of Israel in 40 days would bring about their destruction. More than that, however, they must have believed the gods of their worship were incapable of protecting them. And this meant the God of Israel was not only God in Israel, but everywhere. Indeed, there appears to be little doubt that the people of Nineveh came to faith in the one true God by responding to the limited light given them, not unlike Rahab in Joshua 2 who had heard about how God "dried up the water of the Red sea" for Israel when they "came out of Egypt." (Joshua 2:10) We note that Rahab unquestionably came to faith and was delivered of the impending doom of Jericho. In the roll call of the hall of fame of faith, we read: "By faith the harlot Rahab perished not with them that believed not, when she had received the spies with peace." (Hebrews 11:31) Similarly, we will see in chapter 4 that God delivered the people of Nineveh from the destruction pronounced through Jonah. They, like Rahab, came to faith. (Matthew 12:41) Jonah's preaching, contrary to all he hoped for, accomplished God's purposes. That this revival was genuine is bolstered by the fact that God did not bring judgment on Nineveh until the next century, following the prophetic ministry of Nahum.

Sometimes the significance of what transpired is missed on the modern audience. God's people in Israel were the recipients of tremendous special revelation. As Paul said of Old Testament Israel, "unto them were committed the oracles of God." (Romans 3:2) They had Amos, Elijah, Hosea and other prophets providing God's Word to them in abundance, and characteristically they rejected it and continued in prolonged rebellion. In contrast, the people of Nineveh were pagans, who knew little or nothing of Jehovah, who had no prophets of God to teach them, no oracles of God to learn, and yet at the simple preaching of a five-word message, a city-wide revival ensued. Jonah, as representative of Israel, rejected God's directive in Jonah 1 and rebelled. Yet every other character in the story obeyed the will of God, including the barbaric **people of Nineveh**. (e.g., Nahum 3:1, "woe to the bloody city! It is all full of lies and robbery...") Their seemingly instant repentance on the hearing of minimal revelation from God was a scathing commentary on Israel's refusal to repent in the face of substantial revelation. This is what Jesus had in mind when he scolded the scribes and Pharisees who rejected him, accused him of performing signs by the power of Satan, and demanded a sign: "The men of Nineveh shall rise in judgment with this generation, and shall condemn it: because they repented at the preaching of Jonas; and, behold, a greater than Jonas is here." (Matthew 12:41)

Moreover, since the unfolding of events in Jonah is a prophetic didactic narrative to Israel, we must ask whether the warning to the **people of Nineveh** was put before the people of Israel as a warning to them as well. In my view, the warning to the **people of Nineveh** that **Yet forty days, and Nineveh shall be overthrown** was most probably intended to convey to Israel that "Yet forty **years** and Israel shall be overthrown." Indeed, assuming Jonah preached to Nineveh around 759 BC, forty years later would be approximately the time when Israel was overthrown by the Assyrians (that event occurred in 722 BC). Similarly, when Jesus applied the message of Jonah to his audience, once again, the judgment came approximately 40 years later, when the Romans attacked Jerusalem in AD 70.

We need to be careful, however, at throwing stones at Jonah or Israel insofar as we in the United States today (and much of the world) have more revelation than Israel had in Jonah's day. We too easily take for granted the blessing of having the completed cannon readily available to us. Many of us have a Bible or several Bibles, as well as access to strong teaching from local churches and other ministries (e.g., radio preaching, local Bible college). Yet, by any balanced assessment, our nation is a prodigal nation, and sadly some of our churches are prodigal churches that casted away the Word of God in exchange for worldly conformity, and many professing Christians have little concern for the things of God where it would require genuine life change. Thus, the response of the **people of Nineveh** speaks to us as well, much as it did for Jonah and Israel. We should not want to be the recipient of the scolding Jesus gave the scribes and Pharisees. Yet, we deceive ourselves if we think we can reject (or ignore) God's Word with impunity. "Be not deceived; God is not mocked: for whatsoever a man soweth, that shall he also reap." (Galatians 6:7)

We should also take note of the power of God's Word faithfully proclaimed. There have always been people that want to change the message to make it more palatable by the rapidly changing cultural standards. In modern times, some churches are importing the world's marketing techniques. These folks are cavalier about the Word of God, and in making church a place of entertainment, the Bible has become no more than a prop on the stage and the preacher a purveyor of theological snake oil. This builds nurseries, not effective churches. We need to teach and preach the Word in love and gentleness and meekness, but always in truth (Ephesians 4:15). Then leave the results to God. We should not be surprised by the favorable response of the people of Nineveh, but we will never see that type of revival giving people our words and not God's Word.

> 6 For word came unto the king of Nineveh, and he arose from his throne, and he laid his robe from him, and covered *him* with sackcloth, and sat in ashes. 7 And he caused *it*

> to be proclaimed and published through
> Nineveh by the decree of the king and his
> nobles, saying, Let neither man nor beast,
> herd nor flock, taste any thing: let them not
> feed, nor drink water: <u>8</u> But let man and beast
> be covered with sackcloth, and cry mightily
> unto God: yea, let them turn every one from
> his evil way, and from the violence that *is* in
> their hands.

We are told that the **word** Jonah preached **came unto the king of Nineveh** (probably Ashur-Dan III), who like the rest of the city, responded in repentance. **[H]e arose from his throne**, leaving a place of exaltation to be abased as **he laid his** royal **robe from him, and covered** himself **with sackcloth, and sat in ashes.** The revival that started with the common people worked its way up to the king. And what the people already embraced, the king made into law, causing **it to be proclaimed and published through Nineveh by the decree** (or law) **of the king and his nobles, saying, Let neither man nor beast, herd nor flock, taste any thing: let them not feed, nor drink water.** By these words, the new law required a fast, not only among the people but the animals. Moreover, the decree continued, **But let man and beast be covered with sackcloth, and cry mightily unto God.** Thus, in addition to fasting, everyone was required to pray (plead) to God, by implication, for forgiveness so that perhaps God would not bring judgment on the city. And the decree continued, **yea, let them turn every one from his evil way, and from the violence that is in their hands.** Thus, unlike Jonah's prayer in chapter 2, the people of Nineveh sought deliverance but also forgiveness while demonstrating true repentance. Also, note that some commentators debate the significance of the phrase **and his nobles** as part of the question of whether the

king is the **king** of Assyria or merely a ruler over Nineveh. The question is whether a weakened **king** of Assyria needed his nobles' support, or perhaps a merely local city-wide ruler needed their support. Of course, it may simply be that the text refers to **his nobles** to emphasize the scope of the revival from the least to the greatest. In any event, the issue is not significant to the message of the book, but as demonstrated in the introductory notes, there is good reason to take the phrase **king of Nineveh** to refer to the **king of** Assyria.

Notice their response. Israel never had a good king who pursued God in characteristic obedience, but instead a succession of kings who continued in the "sins of Jeroboam." And generally, as was the king, so were the people. In contrast, and in response to minimal revelation, the **king of Nineveh** repented with his **nobles** and proclaimed a time of fasting, mourning and prayer. These pagans were genuinely convicted and broken about their sin and pleaded to God with contrite hearts—all of which should have been true of Israel. We must ask why Israel with all of its blessings from God could not do the same? And what about the United States? We have moments of silence, but the Ninevites **cry mightily unto God**. To the prodigal nations, churches and people, the book of Jonah holds up the people of Nineveh and loudly demands, "what's your excuse?" They set aside pride, that great enemy of man, and humbled themselves. And notice that unlike Jonah, who never repented, the Ninevites acknowledged their sin and determined to change.

> 9 Who can tell *if* God will turn and repent, and turn away from his fierce anger, that we perish not? 10 And God saw their works, that they turned from their evil way; and God repented of the evil, that he had said that he would do unto them; and he did *it* not.

The king had no disbelief about the veracity of the warning preached by Jonah. He perceived that, because of the warning and the 40 days before the destruction, **God** may **turn and repent, and turn away from his fierce anger, so that we perish not**. The king hoped **God** was merciful. We may ask the question, was their repentance genuine? The necessary conclusion from the context is a resounding "yes" because God did, in fact, **turn away from his fierce anger**. This verse reminds us that the notion of **repent** is to change one's mind, and in this context, it is the hope that God will **repent** or change His mind concerning the pronounced judgment. We read that **God saw their works, that they turned from their evil way**. It is not just the fasting, sackcloth and prayers, but the people **turned from their** sin. As noted previously, sometimes God has to draw us a picture to get through to us. The Ninevites' demonstration of repentance and turning from sin is that picture for Jonah and Israel. It is because of their genuine turning from sin that **God repented** (changed His mind) about **the evil** or destruction that was pronounced.

Someone might ask how an all-knowing God could change His mind? In other words, since God surely knew before Jonah preached what their response would be, how could He have really changed His mind about the destruction? Probably, we are to understand such statements as anthropomorphisms, the projection of a human quality or characteristic onto God to aid our comprehension. The point simply is that God relented, but not arbitrarily. He relented because the people of Nineveh changed course. God relented of the destruction **that he had said that he would do unto them; and he did it not**. The Ninevites' actions show that people can change. The proclamation of the Word of God is about changed lives. The Word is living

– it is able to do, able to accomplish, able to convict, refine, and restore. (Hebrews 4:12; 2 Timothy 3:16) We should never underestimate the power of the message we have to share about the provision of salvation God made for sinners. Recall Paul's words: "But we have this treasure in earthen vessels, that the excellency of the power may be of God, and not of us." (2 Corinthians 4:7)

Closing

For some people, life is a costume party. There is the real person they are and the person we see and hear. Jesus admonished the scribes and Pharisees as "hypocrites! for ye are like unto whited sepulchres, which indeed appear beautiful outward, but are within full of dead men's bones, and of all uncleanness." (Matthew 23:27) Their outward piety was a costume hiding the deadness within. The fact is that it is not difficult to fool people about what is within the heart, but there is no fooling God. Jonah wore the costume of an obedient prophet in chapter 3, but there was no obedience in his heart. As Christians, we must avoid hypocrisy at all costs. There is no room for costume Christianity. What is seen must flow from what really is. We need to do the right thing with the right heart motivations. Anything less fails to please God.

Application Points

- **MAIN PRINCIPLE:** God often brings us to the circumstance of our failure to ready us for our restoration.

- Our external obedience should flow from a faithful heart.

Discussion Questions

1. Why might God bring us back to the circumstances of our failure to make a way for our restoration?

2. Why do you think Jonah's preaching was so effective with the people of Nineveh?

3. Should we expect to see similar revivals today? Why or why not?

4. What is the significance to the animals participating in the mourning by wearing sackcloth and fasting?

5. Should Christians fast, and if so, how? When? And for what purpose?

6. What are the necessary elements of a genuine repentance and turning to God?

Chapter 5

Jonah's Angry Heart

Someone rightly said there are three sides to every issue. In popular thinking, however, there are two sides. One is an Arminian or a Calvinist. One is a Democrat or a Republican. Everything is a choice between the two extremes. But so often a third option is ignored or unseen. In formal logic, this is known as the fallacy of limited choice. Jonah's mindset was dominated by limited choice. Either Nineveh would be destroyed or they would be a threat to Israel. Even if we cannot see the third side, it is a sad state of affairs when we decide that if we cannot see the third side, there is none. God always holds aces. The third side in Jonah's day was that God would deliver the people of Nineveh and deliver Israel, in response to both repenting. To make things worse, when Jonah did not get his way based on his understanding of reality, he became angry and defiant, even to the point of rebuking God. And while most of us might never articulate such defiance to God, we too can feel trapped by our circumstances, unable to see the third side to the issue, then get angry at God. To anyone who was ever angry at God, chapter 4 of the book of Jonah has something to say about an infinitely wise God of love and mercy.

Outline

JONAH'S ANGRY HEART (ch. 4)
- a. Angry Jonah wants to die (4:1-3)
- b. God interrogates Jonah (4:4)
- c. Jonah loves his gourd (4:5-6)
- d. God takes Jonah's gourd (4:7)
- e. Angry Jonah wants to die (4:8)
- f. God intervenes for Jonah (4:9-11)

Scripture and Comments

We have seen God provide Jonah an opportunity to obey in chapter 1, an opportunity to repent in chapter 2, and an opportunity for restoration in chapter 3. This closing chapter of Jonah leaves no question that to this point Jonah's heart remained rebellious. Rather than finding contriteness as we might expect given what happened so far, we find the prophet Jonah, whose public profession is that "I fear the LORD, the God of heaven....," with an increasingly hardened heart. If there has been movement, that movement went from rebellion to livid anger. Indeed, we will see God twice confront Jonah explicitly about his angry heart, "Doest thou well to be angry?" (Jonah 4:4, 9) God is longsuffering (e.g., Exodus 34:6, Numbers 14:18) but not forever-suffering when it comes to chronic disobedience. Eventually there is a last chance to repent. Eventually God closes the door to the ark and the flood rains come. That is where we find the prophet Jonah in this closing chapter, and by implication, the original audience of the divine object lesson—the nation Israel. Now it's game time. The clock is counting down and time is short.

Jonah 4:1 But it displeased Jonah exceedingly, and he was very angry. 2 And he prayed unto the LORD, and said, I pray thee, O LORD, *was* not this my saying, when I was yet in my country? Therefore I fled before unto Tarshish: for I knew that thou *art* a gracious God, and merciful, slow to anger, and of great kindness, and repentest thee of the evil. 3 Therefore now, O LORD, take, I beseech thee, my life from me; for *it is* better for me to die than to live.

Jesus said, "joy shall be in heaven over one sinner that repenteth, more than over ninety and nine just persons, which need no repentance." (Luke 15:7) We witnessed exactly that in Jonah 3 when the people of Nineveh, from the greatest to the least, repented. And such is the heart of God that there is joy in heaven over this. But was there joy in the heart of Jonah? The text says **it displeased Jonah exceedingly, and he was very angry**. What was joy in heaven made Jonah **angry**. The word **angry** translates the Hebrew *charah*, which according to Strong's means "to glow or grow warm; figuratively (usually) to blaze up, of anger, zeal, jealousy:--be angry, burn, displeased, earnestly, fret self, grieve, be (wax) hot, be incensed, kindle, very, be wroth." Jonah was red hot with anger and that anger was directed at God. Ironically, Jonah was not **angry** because his message fell on deaf ears, but because it was well received. We are now told precisely why Jonah did not want to go to Nineveh—he did not want God to show mercy on the Ninevites. The "dove" desperately wanted those sinners to die horrible deaths. He wanted another Sodom and Gomorrah. As referenced in the preface, the Assyrians presented a clear and present danger to Israel, and ultimately, in 722 BC, under the rule of Shalmaneser V and then Sargon II, Assyria defeated Israel. While we may understand apprehension on the part of Jonah, the rebelliousness of Jonah ran far deeper than apprehension or fear.

Jonah's prayer **unto the LORD** expressed his rebuke of God: **I pray thee, O LORD, was not this my saying, when I was yet in my country?** We all understand the phrase, "I told you so." When someone warns us of the consequences of certain actions and we do what we were warned not to do, we may later hear those four painful words, "I told you so." In this case, it was not God telling his prophet those words, but the prophet telling God, "I told you so." The words of Jonah were not included in the limited dialogue of chapter 1, but we are now advised that before Jonah ran from God's presence, he rebuked God about how misguided His plan of preaching to the Ninevites was. (compare Peter's rebuke of Jesus in Matthew 16:22-23) Jonah confessed that he so disagreed with God's plan that he **fled before unto Tarshish: for I knew that thou art a gracious God, and merciful, slow to anger, and of great kindness, and repentest thee of the evil.** Jonah **fled** because he was afraid that if the Ninevites were warned of impending judgment, they might repent and plead for forgiveness, to which the God of heaven, who is **gracious...and merciful...and of great kindness**, would **repentest** (i.e., change His mind) concerning **the evil** or judgment pronounced, thereby sparing Israel's enemy.

Because God did exactly as Jonah anticipated, he now sought (**therefore now**) for the second time to die, pleading with God, **O LORD, take, I beseech thee, my life from me; for it is better for me to die than to live.** Here again we find that Jonah, as representative for the entire prodigal nation Israel, preferred death to repentance and turning back to God.

Jonah obeyed the command to preach to Nineveh, but was never likeminded with God on the matter. His request for death was in no way noble. Jonah learned, as we read in chapter 1, that he could not run away from God, and so he desired death. Jonah would rather **die** than confront the reality of his rebellious heart and need for repentance, and thus told God death is better than life. The irony of all of this is that Jonah feared God's warning to the Ninevites would result in their repentance and God relenting from temporally judging them, yet Jonah and Israel failed to see their own need for repentance with the certainty that God would relent from the eventual judgment of their disobedience.

> 4 Then said the LORD, Doest thou well to be angry?

In the last three verses, Jonah expressed his anger at God for withdrawing judgment on the Ninevites. What ensued in the remainder of the chapter 4 was God's pursuit of Jonah, who should have learned from the example of the Ninevites. It is difficult to miss seeing much of Cain in the heart attitude of Jonah. Recall from Genesis 3 that Cain and Abel both brought their offerings to God, but we are told that "unto Cain and to his offering [God] had not respect. And Cain was very wroth, and his countenance fell." (Genesis 4:5) The text does not explicitly state why God did not respect Cain's offering, but in Hebrews 11:4 we read, "By faith Abel offered unto God a more excellent sacrifice than Cain, by which he obtained witness that he was righteous, God testifying of his gifts: and by it he being dead yet speaketh." The difference between the two brothers' offerings seems to be that one was by faith and the other mere rote. The offering, without a proper attitude of worship and reverence to God as the ultimate provider of all that they have, was empty. And rather than examining his own heart motivations, Cain became angry and directed that anger at Abel. God asked him the same question He asked Jonah, "Why art thou wroth?" (Genesis 4:6) God also provided advice and a warning: "if thou doest well, shalt thou not be accepted? And if thou doest not well, sin lieth at the door. And unto thee shall be his desire, and thou shalt rule over him." (Genesis 4:7) God told Cain the source of his unhappiness was his own heart motivations in the matter of the sacrifice, and that if he did not deal with his heart, sin waits at the door to take control—which we know ultimately happened, with the result that Cain murdered Abel.

The word "well" in both Genesis 4:7 and Jonah 4:4 is the Hebrew *yawtab* and has the sense of doing right. So here in Jonah 4:4, the probing question God asks—**Doest thou well to be angry?**—pointed Jonah to his own heart, and rhetorically demanded a negative answer, for everything up to this point proved Jonah was not doing right by God. And what is also clear is that Jonah's disobedience was not out of ignorance of God's will. Jonah knew what God required of him, and simply chose disobedience. So also the nation of Israel had ample revelation of the will of God, yet openly and deliberately rebelled. Our own United States likewise has ample revelation from God—meaning ready access to the completed canon of Holy Scriptures and Bible teaching churches and schools—yet generally persists in open rebellion. The mirror that the book of Jonah holds up to us is not applicable just to ancient Israel, but present day America too.

> 5 So Jonah went out of the city, and sat on the east side of the city, and there made him a booth, and sat under it in the shadow, till he might see what would become of the city.

Jonah never answered God's question, and we see in verse 5 that he still manifested a hardened heart. Jesus commanded us to love others as we love ourselves. It has been well said that we do not need to learn to love ourselves first—we already have a PhD in loving ourselves. Jonah is no different. The Ninevites were worried whether or not God would destroy them. They were desperate and terrified. Jonah, on the other hand, **went out of the city, and sat on the east side of the city, and there made him a booth, and sat under it in the shadow.** Jonah fashioned himself a hut to shelter him from the hot sun while he watched the fireworks. In other words, Jonah focused on his personal comfort. The Israel of Jonah's day was, like Jonah, quite self-centered. God had blessed them materially and rather than responding to God favorably, their hearts drew further away. Rather than a heart of gratitude to the God who provided in abundance, they pursued wealth to the point of oppression and injustice against the poor, and thanked the gods that are not gods for the blessing they enjoyed.

This verse provides a sad commentary on the heart of Jonah, and unfortunately, some Christians. The world needs the light of truth. In the famous Sermon on the Mount, Jesus exhorted his disciples, "Ye are the light of the world. A city that is set on an hill cannot be hid." (Matthew 5:14) Yet far too many have joined Jonah in finding personal comfort and do not inconvenience themselves for the sake of the gospel. God never intended that we be passive observers only. But Jonah's heart was more than mere apathy. Instead, he was hopeful that God might yet destroy the Ninevites. God vigorously pursued Jonah despite his rebellious heart. Yet Jonah wanted the Ninevites to get justice and not mercy. Jonah found his seat in the theater **till he might see what**

would become of the city. His heart remained unchanged. It is a testimony to the grace of God that He continued chasing rebellious Jonah.

> 6 And the LORD God prepared a gourd, and made *it* to come up over Jonah, that it might be a shadow over his head, to deliver him from his grief. So Jonah was exceeding glad of the gourd. 7 But God prepared a worm when the morning rose the next day, and it smote the gourd that it withered. 8 And it came to pass, when the sun did arise, that God prepared a vehement east wind; and the sun beat upon the head of Jonah, that he fainted, and wished in himself to die, and said, *It is* better for me to die than to live.

Throughout the unfolding of Jonah's rebellion, God pursued him. But here, the approach changed as God employed a divine object lesson. Jonah sought personal comfort, and now God would bless Jonah with additional comfort just as He had blessed Israel with material wealth in Jonah's time. Insofar as Jonah is representative of Israel, and Jonah received undeserved mercy in the form of the comfort and shade provided by the **gourd** for a short time, the plant represents the reign of Jeroboam II (793-753 BC) during which Jonah ministered and during which Israel experienced historic prosperity. That prosperity should have driven Israel to turn in gratitude to their provider God, but it did not. Instead, they did not see beyond the prosperity, as Jonah did not see beyond the plant. The text says **the LORD God prepared a gourd, and made it to come up over Jonah, that it might deliver him from his grief**, in other words, so it could shade **Jonah** from the heat.

I note that some debate about what sort of plant God used here, but the fact is we are not told what type of gourd. Anecdotally, the gourds (i.e., squash) we grow here in southeast and east Texas grow remarkably fast and a budding squash may be ready for the grill in as little as a day or two depending on the conditions; no Jewish reader would be too surprised about a rapidly growing gourd. But even if this is just a common plant, God worked a miracle to make it grow at a supernatural rate to bring Jonah almost immediate comfort from the burning heat of the sun. God **prepared** the **gourd** in the same way that He prepared the great fish. It is due to these recorded supernatural acts that the critics so malign the book, but simply rejecting the supernatural as an axiom is not scholarship. This is not the place for a defense of the supernatural, but I must point out that if the God we worship cannot **prepare** a great fish, a **gourd**, or a worm, likely He cannot resurrect the dead either! As Paul exclaimed, "And if Christ be not risen, then is our preaching vain, and your faith is also vain...ye are yet in your sins" (1 Corinthians 15:14, 17) But rest assured, the death and resurrection of Jesus Christ was the pivotal event in history, it happened in accordance with God's will precisely as set forth in His inspired Word, and nothing was left to happenstance. Here, too, God's pursuit of Jonah was deliberate, precise and powerful.

Hear Jonah's response to the **gourd**: **So Jonah was exceeding glad of the gourd.** Jonah's anger turned to exceeding gladness, not over the mighty hand of God among the Ninevites, but for the personal comfort of a **gourd**. Importantly, we must note that Jonah did not give God praise or thanks for the **gourd**. Truly, how far Jonah's heart was from God. In the same way, Israel enjoyed God's blessing during the reign of Jeroboam II, yet did not credit God or honor Him with obedience. To try to reach Jonah, God removed the **gourd** almost as quickly as He raised it up. God made the **gourd**, as He did all of creation, and thus He was free to do with the gourd as it pleased Him. As with the fish and the gourd, **God prepared a worm when the morning rose the next day, and it smote** or ate **the gourd that it withered**. Historically, Jeroboam II's reign ended in 753 BC, and he was succeeded by Zechariah, but Zechariah was murdered by Shallum that same year, abruptly ending the dynasty of Jehu after four generations, as was prophesied (2 Kings 10:30). If the **gourd** represented Jeroboam's reign, then the **worm** was predictive of God's ending the dynasty of Jehu, and Israel's prosperity, in the near future.

However, the **worm** was only step one to God removing Jonah's personal comfort. Step two, as **it came to pass, when the sun did arise** and presumably after God removed the **gourd, God prepared a vehement east wind**. Strong, hot winds usually came from the east, and that brought the heat to Jonah first since he was on the east side of the city. The use of a strong east wind is usually associated with the action (and often judgment) of God. (e.g., Genesis 41:6, 23, 27; Exodus 10:13, 14:21) While Jonah was focused on Nineveh and hoping God would destroy it, God was focused on Jonah and the events here were again predictive. The **gourd** is the prosperous reign of Jeroboam, which the **worm** brought to an end. Should Israel not repent and turn back to God, then the **east wind** of judgment would be used of God on Israel just as the **vehement east wind** came against Jonah. Ironically in light of the experiences of Jonah that we witness in this chapter of his book, that **east wind** came from none other than the Assyrians.

Jonah, however, did not accept the will of God with regard to the **gourd,** the **worm** or the **east wind** any more than he did with regard to the Ninevites. Jonah truly reached spiritual rock bottom. For the loss of the **gourd** and some hot weather, he wanted (yet again) to die. We read that **the sun beat upon the head of Jonah, that he fainted, and wished in himself to die, and said, It is better for me to die than to live.** Without the slightest concern for the Ninevites, Jonah fainted of life because he lost his shade and a hot wind blew through. His sense of being was now wholly tied to the creation and not his relationship to the Creator. Throughout the book, Jonah responded to God by fleeing or attempting to flee, but God limited his ability to do so. Here again Jonah was pushed to a decision, and he preferred death to repentance. If this sounds absurd to you, it should. That's the point! The nation Israel would rather perish than turn to God and that thinking is insane.

The embarrassing behavior of Jonah in this chapter was a convicting object lesson for Israel, and Jonah's desire for death over repentance—just as in chapter 1 when he besought the sailors to toss him overboard—tragically foreshadowed the decision Israel would make. As already indicated, the death Israel embraced to avoid repentance came at the hands of the Assyrians, the people that include the Ninevites. But if God could take out Nineveh, He could have held the Assyrians at bay or destroyed them to protect Israel, which God actually did to protect Judah when the Assyrians attempted to take Jerusalem much later. Israel could not see the irrationality of their decision so God held up Jonah— also too stiff-necked to see reality—to draw them a picture. And by application, rebellious Jonah is on display before us. Do we love the gourd more than people? Where is our heart? And are we like Jonah fleeing God in some area of our lives, some area where we are not likeminded with God?

9 And God said to Jonah, Doest thou well to be angry for the gourd? And he said, I do well to be angry, *even* unto death. 10 Then said the LORD, Thou hast had pity on the gourd, for the which thou hast not laboured, neither madest it grow; which came up in a night, and perished in a night: 11 And should not I spare Nineveh, that great city, wherein are more than sixscore thousand persons that cannot discern between their right hand and their left hand; and *also* much cattle?

These three verses bring us to the end of the story that is intentionally no ending at all. God's next question for Jonah is like the one in verse 4, but it is narrowed to make a point. God asked Jonah, **Doest thou well to be angry for the gourd?** The question is rhetorical, designed to make Jonah consider his attitude and how his anger stemmed from the loss of the **gourd**. But Jonah would not hear such criticism, even from God, and quipped, **I do well to be angry, even unto death**. Jonah said he was the righteous one, and his anger was righteous. Jonah says he was not only **well** or right **to be angry**, but that he was willing to die (**even unto death**) for his position, which he is also **well** or right to persist in. This anger was obviously about more than the **gourd**. Perhaps at this point, Jesus' words to the Pharisees are applicable: "If ye were blind, ye should have no sin: but now ye say, We see; therefore your sin remaineth." (John 9:41)

Jonah placed the fault with God and remained blind to his hardened, rebellious heart. In the first chapter, Jonah claimed to fear God, but since then his vain rhetoric has been shown for what it is. Indeed, between chapter 1 and this point in Jonah's story, the true depth of his hardheartedness was revealed. In truth, Jonah acknowledged God but wanted nothing of God except deliverance from the perils of life, and in particular, denounced God's authority over him and God's standards. Jonah instead embraced what felt right to him, even murderous anger toward the Ninevites now directed at God, and Jonah will persist on this path even if it means death. So once again, given the choice, Jonah (and by implication Israel) chose death to repentance.

God's response called out the moral absurdity of Jonah's behavior and cut right to the heart of the matter: **Thou hast had pity on the gourd, for the which thou hast not labored, neither madest it grow; which came up in a night, and perished at night: And should I not spare Nineveh, that great city, wherein are more than sixscore** or 120,000 **persons that cannot discern between their right hand and their left hand; and also much cattle?** Jonah loved the **gourd** but not the Ninevites. God's initial question was designed to bring that out. There was no particular reason for Jonah to mourn the loss of the **gourd** as he had nothing to do with its existence or growth. It was just a plant and was very temporary. But God loved the Ninevites, whom He planted and watered, and if Jonah so loved the gourd, how much more should God love the people of Nineveh. God appealed to Jonah to be likeminded. For if Jonah could be so easily stirred to have passion for the plant, then why not for the people of **Nineveh, that great city.**

The meaning of **persons that cannot discern between their right hand and their left hand** has engendered much debate. Some believe God appealed to Jonah to at least have concern for the children of the city. But consistent with the overall message of the book, most probably the reference was to their spiritual ignorance. In contrast to Jonah and Israel, recipients of substantial special revelation from God, the inhabitants of Nineveh were largely ignorant of God and thus had no basis for discernment. The notion is that those with more revelation have a heightened responsibility of obedience. Here, God was telling Jonah that His mercy was appropriate especially in view of Nineveh's spiritual ignorance, to wit, their ignorance that their actions violated God's standards. God even referenced **much cattle** in the city. This again points to the fact that even with the limited revelation provided them through Jonah, they repented and fasted in sackcloth and ashes and incorporated their livestock into the display. God would spare the Ninevites and the animals, both ignorant yet responding (figuratively in the case of the livestock) to the light given them.

What Jonah seemed oblivious to is that if God were to destroy the ignorant Ninevites even after they repented at Jonah's preaching, then that same standard of judgment would have required that He utterly destroy Israel also. Through these events, Israel was called yet again to repentance before their destruction. They are called to witness that the barbaric, spiritually ignorant Ninevites repented. Indeed, even the livestock participated in the outward showing of repentance. As we have seen throughout the book of Jonah, everything and everyone responded to God—be it plant, animal, fish or pagan human—except Jonah. And at this point, the book just stops. This too has engendered much debate. Are we missing verses? Is the book incomplete? Why does it simply stop with God's question?

Every good sermon, in one way or another, brings people to a decision. Some truth or truths are exhorted from the Word of God and the hearer is responsible to acknowledge and act on it. A part of Jonah's life was played out on the screen for all Israel to see. This divine object lesson pulled no punches. That Jonah stood in for Israel and behaved irrationally and rebelliously as Israel was obvious. That God steadfastly pursued Jonah with grace and mercy was equally as obvious. Even ignorant pagans with virtually no revelation from God had the spiritual snap to figure it out and repent, but not Jonah, and not Israel.

What remained for Israel was to step in where the story of Jonah stopped and write how their story ends. The choice, one final time before the destruction—before the east wind comes—was theirs to make. As the saying goes, the ball was in their court. Jonah consistently chose death to repentance but by God's mercy was spared up to the point where the book just stops. Now it is decision time. Now it is time for a verdict. Israel must choose to repent or die. Israel cannot sit on the fence or make no decision, for that itself is to choose death. If we believe Jonah wrote the book (as this author does), then it seems Jonah at some point repented, for a non-repentant Jonah could not write the book the way it is. Sadly, however, we know the ending Israel chose to write was, **I do well to be angry, even unto death.** And so they died at the hands of the Assyrians when they were overtaken in 722 B.C. God is longsuffering but eventually the window of opportunity closed, the clock ran down to zero, and the hammer of God fell on the disobedient.

And what of us? Like Israel, the United States has enjoyed substantial revelation from God and characteristically, at least in recent decades, rejected it. We deceive ourselves to think God winks at our sin while He did not wink at Israel's or Nineveh's. And what of our churches that have largely abandoned the Word of God? They heard God speak but became angry, charting their own worldly course with platitudes of self-assurance for their new direction, while still proclaiming like Jonah that they fear God. And what of you, and what of me? The book of Jonah strips us of our excuses and holds us up to the repentant Ninevites. If we see ourselves in Jonah, then we dare not do anything but turn back to God.

Closing

What a cast of characters. A prodigal prophet, insightful mariners, a tempest, man overboard, a specially prepared fish, *sheol*, a great city, the people of Nineveh, the animals of Nineveh, a gourd plant, a worm and an east wind. And most of all, a God that chases sinners, beckoning them to repent and turn back to Him, a God of grace and mercy, but also a God that preserves our volition and lets us write the ending of the story. If we look at ourselves in the mirror and find nothing of Jonah in us, the book yet speaks to us. For it reveals God's love in action. Looking at God's pursuit of the prodigal prophet, we better understand the One who would send His Son "to seek and to save that which was lost." (Luke 19:10) If the book does not call us to repentance, then it teaches us to love the unlovable. The picture of humanity is not pretty—a prophet who knows God but despises Him, and pagans that know nothing of God and revel in unbridled violence. Yet God's love pursues both, and that should teach all of us, carrying treasure as we do in earthen vessels, good news for a dying world that needs Jesus Christ. To do nothing with the gospel is to fashion a shelter east of the world and wait for the fireworks. But to get with God's program is to pursue the lost with the light of the truth of the gospel. Is it not far past time that we arise and go?

Application Points

- **MAIN PRINCIPLE:** God is longsuffering but the window of opportunity to repent and turn back to Him will eventually close.

- Anger is never a proper response to the will of God.

- No one is beyond the reach of the love of God.

Discussion Questions

1. Why is Jonah so angry at God and what does that reveal about his heart?

2. What indication (if any) is there that Jonah ever repented?

3. Why does Jonah persist in his disobedience in the face of God's clear message that He wishes to deliver the people of Nineveh from destruction?

4. What do we learn about Jonah from his repeated desire for death? How would the same or similar attitudes play out in the life of a Christian today?

5. Do you have any reason to doubt Jonah's salvation? Why or why not?

6. How might our close association (friendship) with mature believers help prevent us from being a Jonah?

7. Can Jonah blame an –ism or addiction for his disobedience?

8. When is it proper for a Christian to point to an –ism or addiction as the source of their disobedience to God?

Bibliography

The following sources were consulted for the writing of this book.

Allen, Leslie C., *The Books of Joel, Obadiah, Jonah, and Micah*, THE NEW INTERNATIONAL COMMENTARY ON THE OLD TESTAMENT, William B. Eerdmans Publishing Company (1976). Portions of this commentary are brilliant, but Mr. Allen views the book as a parable directed at Judah many years after the fall of Nineveh, and at several points this (incorrect) presumption shades his interpretation.

Campbell, Donald K., *The Minor Prophets*, messages on audio cassettes available through the Dallas Theological Seminary's Tape Ministry, www.dts.edu.

Chisholm, Robert B., Jr., *Interpreting the Minor Prophets*, Academic Books (1990). A solid conservative resource with short commentaries on each of the minor prophets.

Deffinbaugh, Robert L., *Jonah: The Prodigal Prophet*, Biblical Studies Press (1998). This is only 29 pages and can be downloaded for free from www.bible.org. Upholds the historicity of Jonah.

DeVries, LaMoine F., *Cities of the Biblical World*, Hendrickson Publishers, Inc. (1997). An excellent and inexpensive reference that has a solid write-up on the 60 most relevant cities in the Bible.

Feinberg, Charles L., *The Minor Prophets*, Moody Publishers (1976). An excellent overview of all of the minor prophets from a Jewish Christian perspective.

Freeman, Hobart E., *An Introduction to the Old Testament Prophets*, Faith Ministries & Publications (2004). An excellent resource with brief commentaries on each of the minor prophets.

Ironside, H. A., *The Minor Prophets*, AN IRONSIDE EXPOSITORY COMMENTARY, Kregal Publications (2004). This is an excellent resource with brief commentaries on each of the minor prophets, originally published in 1904. Upholds the historicity of Jonah.

Loken, Israel P., *The Old Testament Prophetic Books: An Introduction*, Xulon Press (2010). Outstanding overview of all of the prophetic books with excellent historical context, outlines and study questions.

Martin, Hugh, *Jonah*, GENEVA SERIES OF COMMENTARIES, The Banner of Truth Trust (1995). This commentary was first published in 1870 and remains one of the longest, most detailed available, with considerable focus on the theological implications for Christians. Upholds the historicity of Jonah.

McGee, J. Vernon, *Thru the Bible – Proverbs through Malachi*, Thomas Nelson Publishers (1982). This work contains an excellent short commentary on Jonah taken from Mr. McGee's radio addresses. Mr. McGee writes a superb defense of the historicity of Jonah in his introduction. Mr. McGee takes the minority view among conservatives that Jonah died in the fish and was resurrected.

Nixon, Rosemary, *The Message of Jonah*, THE BIBLE SPEAKS TODAY, InterVarsity Press (2003). This is one of the more detailed commentaries now available on Jonah, but the author views Jonah as a parable and that necessarily slants her interpretation at points. This is, however, an excellent and insightful work.

Patterson, Richard D., *Nahum, Habakkuk, Zephaniah*, Biblical Studies Press (2003). This is an outstanding commentary from the head of the Biblical Studies Department at Liberty University.

Smith, Billy K. and Page, Frank S., *Amos, Obadiah, Jonah*, THE NEW AMERICAN COMMENTARY, Broadman & Holman Publishers (1995). An excellent, solid, unapologetically conservative commentary that upholds the historicity of Jonah.

Timmer, Daniel C., *A Gracious and Compassionate God*, NEW STUDIES IN BIBLICAL THEOLOGY, InterVarsity Press (2011). A detailed and scholarly analysis of Jonah.

Toussaint, Stanley, *Exposition of Jonah*, messages on audio cassettes available through the Dallas Theological Seminary's Tape Ministry, www.dts.edu.

Walvoord, John F. and Zuck, Roy B., *The Bible Knowledge Commentary, Old Testament*, ChariotVictor Publishing (1985). Excellent set of brief commentaries on the entire Old Testament in a single volume, all by very conservative writers. The historical background to the books is especially valuable.

About the Author

HUTSON SMELLEY is an attorney and Bible teacher residing in Houston, Texas with his wife and six children. He holds advanced degrees in mathematics, law and Biblical studies. He can be contacted at proclaimtheword@me.com.

www.proclaimtheword.me